OPPORTUNITIES

in

Military Careers

OPPORTUNITIES

in

Military
Careers

REVISED EDITION

ADRIAN A. PARADIS

McGraw-Hill

New York   Chicago   San Francisco   Lisbon   London   Madrid   Mexico City
Milan   New Delhi   San Juan   Seoul   Singapore   Sydney   Toronto

Library of Congress Cataloging-in-Publication Data

Paradis, Adrian A.
　　　Opportunities in military careers / Adrian A. Paradis. — Rev. ed.
　　　　　p.　　cm.
　　　ISBN 0-07-144852-7
　　　1. United States—Armed Forces—Vocational guidance.　　I. Title.

　　UB147.P37　　2005
　　355'.0023'73—dc22　　　　　　　　　　　　　　　　2005004980

3　4　5　6　7　8　9　0　　DOC/DOC　　0　9　8　7　6

ISBN 0-07-144852-7

Interior design by Rattray Design

McGraw-Hill books are available at special quantity discounts to use as premiums and sales promotions, or for use in corporate training programs. For more information, please write to the Director of Special Sales, Professional Publishing, McGraw-Hill, Two Penn Plaza, New York, NY 10121-2298. Or contact your local bookstore.

This book is printed on acid-free paper.

Contents

FOREWORD

YOUNG AMERICAN MEN and women today have a constantly widening and impressive array of career opportunities awaiting them. As a nation, we can be proud of a bright and promising future for our rising generations.

Those future prospects attest to the importance of the professions described in this book. In an uncertain world, history teaches us that the accomplishments of free people must be protected. This lesson is most obvious in time of war or international crisis, but it also applies in times that appear tranquil. Every day Americans in all walks of life can go about their pursuits with confidence because of the contributions of their compatriots who have chosen to dedicate some or all of their professional lives to military service.

Our men and women in the armed forces serve in many capacities at many locations in the United States and around the world. They work in a spectrum of specialties that mirrors opportunities available in American society at large. Many serve in the military for only a few years and then move on to careers in the private sector that are enhanced by the training, experience, and maturity they have acquired. Others remain longer and make uniformed service their lifelong vocation. They follow many paths, but all share in the pride that comes with having done special work to serve their country and to guarantee a secure future for the generations to come.

I hope all readers of this book will carefully consider the challenging opportunities outlined in these pages. For those who choose to join our ranks, I know you will find life in military service rewarding in many ways.

William J. Crowe Jr.
Former Chairman, Joint Chiefs of Staff

INTRODUCTION

REGARDLESS OF WHERE you may be in school, college, or your early working years, if you are concerned about finding a challenging career, look no further—at least until you have reviewed the job prospects in this book.

After you consider the wealth of opportunities revealed here, you may well find the perfect career, making a further search unnecessary. Most of us take the military establishment for granted during peacetime, until an enemy threatens our nation's security; then we look to the men and women in the armed services to protect us and ward off possible harm. This kind of insurance in today's world calls for a vast globe-encircling organization, some of which is on the alert every moment of every hour, every day. It requires an incredibly large number of highly trained personnel in occupations as diverse as piloting airplanes, operating advanced electronic equipment, or manning a radar range-finder, to lesser skilled occupations like carpentry, painting, or cooking. Take your pick from the hundreds of career possibilities, which are all yours for the choosing with free training at Uncle Sam's expense.

Before we proceed further, let us be the first to admit that a career in the military—no matter what it may be—is not for everyone. For various reasons, some young men and women do not want any connection to the armed forces, although they may readily acknowledge their necessity when our country is attacked. However, a large part of the population understands both the importance of the military establishment and the advantages it offers those seeking meaningful careers.

In the civilian world there are few, if any, employment opportunities where you can step into a paying job and receive training. If you have a high school diploma, there are countless opportunities for job training leading to a useful skill that is vital to the service you have chosen and is also valuable later in the outside world, when you retire or elect to leave the military.

The military sometimes describes itself as America's oldest company. In an overview that was published on its official website, http://www.defenselink.mil, the Pentagon says: ". . . if you look at us in business terms, many would say we are not only America's largest company, but its busiest and most successful."

Unlike a business operation, though, the Defense Department is not subject to buyouts, leverages, or the whims of the economy. The military is here to stay—and so are its jobs. In the aftermath of September 11, 2001, the military has intensified its traditional national defense mission, augmenting its capabilities in a number of areas, such as homeland security and defending against weapons of mass destruction. Additionally, the military has continued its humanitarian missions, responding to natural disasters both at home and abroad. None of these missions can be completed without people—which the military employs in huge numbers. In early 2005 the Pentagon reported 1.4 million people on active duty, with another 1.2 million serving in the National Guard and Reserve forces.

The military also offers a number of civilian positions, usually in administrative support jobs. These are similar to openings in private industry, where you must have already acquired the necessary office or other skills to qualify. However, as a civilian employee, you are not entitled to the various services and materials, such as free food, clothing, shelter, and educational and recreational opportunities, that are made available to members of the military.

Because each service offers a great number of job opportunities, it is wise to talk to the nearest recruiting personnel of the services that interest you. They can tell you what openings are available. Keep in mind, however, that it may be necessary to select a second or third job choice should there be nothing in the area you prefer. That is because the employment needs of each service fluctuate as personnel retire or the need for the skill you envision learning is no longer required.

This book will introduce you to each of the four principal services: the Navy, the Marines, the Army, and the Air Force. The order of their appearance was determined by drawing lots, since they are of equal importance to the overall military establishment. The U.S. Coast Guard follows the armed services because it is only during wartime that the Coast Guard becomes an active military organization; its normal responsibilities are of a more peacetime nature. Nevertheless, it is also an important service that offers numerous challenging career opportunities.

Following our introduction to each of the five services, we will discuss several areas of concern to every career-minded person: the advantages and disadvantages of military service, responsibilities assumed, educational opportunities for officer candidates, and related civilian openings. Finally, in the Appendixes, you will find information about military career fields; the duties, responsibilities, and qualifications of each; and examples of related civilian jobs.

If the prospect of earning while learning is music to your ears, read ahead and discover for yourself what career possibilities can be yours.

AN OVERVIEW OF THE ARMED FORCES

IF THE U.S. military were a business, it would be the largest, busiest, and oldest company in America. With roots reaching back to pre-Revolutionary times, the military has operated steadily since 1775.

Like all companies, the American military establishment has evolved over time. At first it consisted of three services: the Army, the Navy, and the Marine Corps. In 1789 the military branches operated under direction of the War Department. In 1947 a new service—the Air Force—split off from the Army. The War Department became the Department of the Army, and the three main services—the Army, Navy, and Air Force—were placed under the control of a newly created secretary of defense. In 1949 the secretary was placed at the helm of a newly formed Department of Defense, with headquarters at the Pentagon.

Today the military is similar to a conglomerate spanning the globe. The American armed forces operate in every time zone and in more than 145 countries around the world. It has an almost incomprehensibly large budget: three-hundred seventy-one *billion* dollars.

Unlike any other company in America, the military is officially assigned a unique responsibility: national defense. This includes fighting wars, counterterrorism, disaster relief, and even humanitarian aid. The overall mission is a vital and unequaled assignment—one that is performed by people.

Who are the people in the military? In October 2001, shortly after the tragic events of September 11, defense secretary Donald Rumsfeld described these people while delivering a message to the troops. In his message, Secretary Rumsfeld said, "You are the sharp sword of freedom."

This does not mean that every member of the armed forces is a warrior. In fact, 80 percent of all military personnel serve in noncombat jobs. They do, however, support those personnel who do the actual fighting. And as any soldier or sailor or airman will affirm, no gun can fire without bullets delivered by a supply officer; no troop can function without food provided by cooks; and no truck can operate without the help of a skilled mechanic. In other words, all military jobs are important.

The jobs are also in plentiful supply. The services currently operate more than three hundred types of schools that offer full-time and part-time training as well as opportunities in more than forty-one hundred military job specialties. Significantly, 88 percent of those jobs have direct civilian counterparts. This means that a thoughtful job seeker would do well to consider the military; not only does the military serve an important purpose to the nation, but it also prepares its members for successful careers both within the armed forces and subsequent civilian life.

The following chapters will address the various military services and related matters in greater depth. But first, let's take a look at some pertinent information, starting with how the armed forces are organized.

Organization of the Armed Forces

The military is run by a complex amalgam of uniformed officers and civilian government officials. The commander-in-chief is the president of the United States. On a broad scale, the president makes major decisions on how to use the armed forces. These decisions are funded and approved (or not approved) by Congress. A primary example would be the decision to go to war.

The National Command Authority, which consists of the president and the secretary of defense, supervises military operations. Does this mean that the president and the secretary of defense are personally involved in every military mission? No. They delegate authority through the Joint Chiefs of Staff, who lead the individual services. This authority then passes through the leaders of the unified multiservice command and downward through the services and their various commands and bases and units.

Most military personnel have little, if any, day-to-day dealings with high-ranking commanders. Most personnel function only within their units, according to their particular service. Although all services share the job of national defense, each approaches the task in a distinct way.

The Army defends the landmass of the United States, along with those of its territories, commonwealths, and possessions. It conducts ground war abroad, fighting in battles and holding territory. It operates in some fifty countries.

The Navy maintains combat-ready seagoing forces that both wage war and deter foreign aggression. It maintains freedom of the seas. It operates in and near hostile waters, ready to provide near-instantaneous combat power, should the need arise. Additionally, the Navy participates in international humanitarian relief efforts.

The Marine Corps is an expeditionary combat force attached to the Navy. It operates via land, air, and sea.

The Air Force performs airborne combat and peacekeeping roles in hot spots around the world. It also takes part in international humanitarian relief.

The Coast Guard enforces federal maritime laws, rescues distressed vessels and aircraft at sea, and prevents smuggling. Normally, the Coast Guard is part of the Transportation Department; however, during war, it operates under the Navy.

People Power

All four services combine to create a huge national defense operation. While it is true that the United States defends itself with a dazzling array of technology and machinery, it is also true that the equipment runs on people power.

The military has about 1.4 million people on active duty, with an additional 1.2 million belonging to National Guard and Reserve forces. Another 654,000 or so civilians also are employed by the military in various functions.

The military is known for its high standards. More than half of the enlisted force has had at least some college experience. The military encourages its members to pursue academic goals and has programs in place to help its members achieve those goals—in some cases, contributing as much as $50,000 in tuition to an individual.

Physical development is also important. Military personnel are encouraged to keep their bodies strong and healthy. Although physical development is important, the armed forces do not expect all members to enter the service in peak athletic form. Potential recruits sometimes fear that physical standards are so high that they will not be able to complete the rigorous basic recruit training. The Pentagon assures us, though, that most young people can meet the standards; approximately 90 percent of new recruits are able to complete the basic training regimen.

The Armed Forces and You

Before pursuing a stint in the armed forces any further, think about what it means to take the military oath of allegiance. That oath reads as follows:

> I do solemnly swear that I will support and defend the Constitution of the United States against all enemies, foreign and domestic; that I will bear true faith and allegiance to the same; and that I will obey the orders of the President of the United States and the orders of the officers appointed over me, according to regulations and the Uniform Code of Military Justice. So help me God.

The military takes this oath seriously and expects you to do the same. If you join one of the services, your first obligation is to become a useful, loyal, and enthusiastic member of that service and give it everything you can during peacetime and wartime. You also will sign a promise that obliges you to complete your term of service. Your commitment will mean that you personally may wind up standing between America and any enemy. This is serious stuff. You should consider it carefully and understand what joining means before you apply for enlistment or a commission. Your commitment should be binding whether or not you agree with our nation's policies on how, when, or where it deploys its troops.

When you enter the military you should have no problems if you are ready to embrace this new way of life that is as honorable and important as any other profession. In time of war or threat from a potential enemy, nothing in our country is as important as the role of the armed services, which may include you. As a member, you could have every reason to be proud of a job that is vital to the success of the entire establishment.

We mention all this because a career in the military is far, far more than learning a trade or profession and holding down a job. It is foremost a solemn and almost sacred responsibility to join with all your associates in a mutual and determined effort to protect our nation. Your military career and that of your fellow soldiers is what makes the goal possible. Your most important reason for becoming an airman, soldier, sailor, or Marine is to protect our country in time of peril.

2

THE NAVY

"JOIN THE NAVY and See the World!" was a familiar recruiting poster that appeared on the streets in many cities and towns. Some of the other services had similar posters encouraging young men to enlist and serve their country. Doubtless many Americans imagined themselves in uniform serving in some capacity on the high seas or at a fascinating post overseas.

Evolution of Navies

No one knows when the first navy, as such, made its appearance. It is thought that as tribes and then nations began trading, people used their primitive boats not only for fishing and transporting goods, but also as transport into battle. The existence of the so-called rowing galleys as early as 2000 B.C. or even earlier is confirmed in carvings found in Egyptian tombs and the writings of Homer. Such ships had a displacement of perhaps twenty tons and held as many as fifty or more rowers. Although improvements were made in the design and construction of these craft, they did not change materially for some twenty-five hundred years. They were used by all of the nations bordering on the Mediterranean, as well as by the Vikings to the north. The last important sea battle that was fought between rowing galleys was the climax of a long naval duel between the Spaniards and Turks. It took place on October 7, 1571, off Lepanto, Greece. By this time most of these ships measured some 140 feet in length, displaced about 170 tons, and were manned by crews of more than 200 men, 150 of whom were rowers.

Although galleys were used as late as Napoleon's time, most nations with seacoasts had long begun to develop warships using sails. As interest in discovery grew during the fifteenth century, explorers found that the sailing ships enabled them to make longer and faster voyages. In the sixteenth century, the English decided to devote an entire deck of a sailing ship to small cannon. Later, the British installed guns on three decks, resulting in formidable battleships. Naval architecture and battle tactics remained practically unchanged until after 1800, when three developments revolutionized warfare at sea:

1. The newly perfected steam engine was used first to drive a paddle wheel and later a screw propeller.
2. Iron and steel replaced wood, making it possible to build larger and stronger ships.
3. The invention of the explosive shell made it possible to sink a ship if it were struck at waterline or below. These shells were later followed by mines, torpedoes, bombs, and, finally, guided missiles.

The American Navy had its beginning near the end of the era of sailing ships.

The United States Navy

The Continental Navy was established in 1775 to serve during the Revolutionary War. However, after the Peace of Paris in 1783, the ships were sold. It was not until 1794 that Congress voted to build six frigates to fight the Barbary pirates. In 1797 the United States Navy was launched. The following year the office of Secretary of the Navy was created. The role the Navy played in the War of 1812 enabled it to establish itself as an important part of the nation's defense forces.

Meanwhile, the new navy had acquired its first steam-driven warship, the U.S.N. *Fulton*. By the end of the Civil War, this navy was the largest and most powerful force in the world. When the Spanish-American War erupted, the navy easily wiped out the ten Spanish battleships that opposed it.

This victory occurred about ten years after Alfred Thayer Mahan had published two books on the influence of sea power. He was a naval officer who had served in the Civil War and later lectured on naval history and strategy at the Naval War College in Newport, Rhode Island. Mahan pointed out that success in international politics and economics depended on naval power. This was because the nation that controlled the seas became the dominant country in time of war and peace. As a result, many countries built up their sea power.

President Theodore Roosevelt and other national leaders became convinced that a strong navy was essential. Following up on the recent victorious war with Spain, in 1907 the president sent four destroyers and sixteen battleships on a fourteen-month world cruise, aiming to impress other nations with America's sea power. The ships were painted white to add to the impressiveness of the occasion. They became known as The Great White Fleet.

Mighty battleships dominated the seas until after World War I. However, wartime operations of the airplane caused a profound change in the Navy during the 1920s. Back in 1910 Eugene Ely had made the first flight from a ship, the cruiser *Birmingham*. The following year the Navy purchased its first airplane. In 1914 the Naval Air Station in Pensacola, Florida, was established, and the original aircraft carrier, *Langley*, set sail in 1922. Thereafter, the aircraft carrier was to take the place of the warship with its mighty guns, and the carrier's superiority was soon to be proven. When the Japanese attacked Pearl Harbor on December 7, 1941, the Navy had several huge flattops, but fortunately none were lost in that initial attack.

Seven months later, following one American defeat after another, the Battle of Midway was fought from June 3 to June 6, proving one of the most decisive engagements of World War II. In this conflict, American planes sank four Japanese aircraft carriers and crippled the enemy's navy. This ended the invasion threat. The enemy began its long retreat toward its homeland. Oddly enough, although two large naval fleets were pitted against each other, no ships engaged in battle; fighter planes and bombers from aircraft carriers did all the fighting.

Since the end of World War II, the Navy has undergone tremendous change. Its submarines have become among the nation's most important defensive weapons carriers. Furthermore, the advent of hydrogen bombs, development of nuclear power, and the vulnerability of ships to attack by aircraft or guided missiles have transformed the Navy into one of the most exciting of the armed services.

The Navy Today

The Navy's main mission is to protect the United States. It is a sea-based, forward-deployed force that serves as a major deterrent to foreign aggression. With its massive aircraft carriers and arsenal of combat aircraft, the Navy in effect provides mobile military bases to hot spots around the world.

The Navy owns some 289 ships and 4,000 aircraft. As of January 2005, the service was nearly 372,000 members strong. Of that number, about 54,000 were officers and about 313,500 were enlisted. The occupational fields open to officers and enlisted personnel are discussed later in Appendix A. Meanwhile, let's take a look at the Navy itself.

Naval Operating Forces

Naval forces are organized under a number of commands such as Military Sealift Command, U.S. Naval Forces Europe, or the Atlantic and Pacific Fleets. The operational, seagoing Navy is housed at massive bases on the coasts of the U.S. mainland, Hawaii, and abroad; but the ships themselves go anywhere the country needs them to be, such as the Far East, the Persian Gulf, or the Mediterranean Sea.

Over the years the Navy has developed a number of specialized ships, each for a specific purpose. Thus there are guided missile cruisers that escort the huge aircraft carriers. There are destroyers defending battleships and other warships. There are frigates (smaller than cruisers and larger than destroyers) that escort other warships and patrol coastlines. In addition, there are submarines that carry guided missiles, operate against surface ships or other submarines, and function in shore positions; there are also command ships, which are floating administrative headquarters.

There are also various auxiliary ships. Fleet support craft maintain and tow other ships. Replenishment ships bring fuel, food, ammunition, and spare parts to the fleet. The sealift ships carry cargo from port to port. Experimental research ships aid in developing and testing ships, weapons, and equipment. Surveying ships map coastlines and the ocean floor.

Not to be overlooked is the naval fleet of aircraft. There are cargo, observation, patrol, antisubmarine, and training planes, as well as helicopters. Finally, there are the Navy's ordnance weapons. These are bombs, guns, mines, torpedoes, and missiles. Its eight-inch cannon hurl shells as far as seventeen miles. Most powerful and awesome of all weapons is the missile in the Trident submarine, which has a range of four thousand miles and enough explosive power to level a huge city.

This is a short overview of our Navy. Now to the most interesting part of all—where you might fit into the picture.

What's in It for You?

Water, air, or land—no matter which appeals to you, there is something for everyone. Countless jobs in a variety of environments are available to those interested in a career with the Navy.

On the Sea

Skimming the calm, clear seas or plowing through thundering waves, the Navy's surface ships are ready for action. They're powerful destroyers, frigates, and big-gun battleships that sail with the huge aircraft carriers. These ships offer hundreds of exciting jobs in a variety of technical fields.

The Navy has dozens of sizes and types of surface ships. Each ship has a specific mission that could take you anywhere in the world. Not only will you become an expert seaman and a worldwide traveler in the Navy, you'll get paid for the training and adventure, too.

Down Below

Under the ocean's surface, a Navy submarine glides through the quiet darkness. All eyes in the control room are on the sonar visual display, watching for any approaching ships. As a submariner, you'll serve aboard a ship as modern and complex as any to be found in the Navy. The purity of the air you breathe when submerged is scientifically controlled, and temperature and humidity are adjusted for comfort. It's a unique lifestyle that offers extra pay if you qualify to be part of it.

Above the Ocean

Soaring through the clouds high above the earth's surface, a Navy jet flashes past faster than the speed of sound. Maintaining the sophisticated machinery that keeps that Navy jet in the air is an extremely important, satisfying, and responsible job that calls for expert training in a highly technical field. That skill is taught in the Navy.

You'll thrill to the excitement as a Navy plane catapults skyward from the deck of an aircraft carrier at sea—then watch with pride when it's skillfully landed back aboard ship. You'll be one of the six thousand crew members living aboard a Navy aircraft carrier—one of the world's largest ships.

On Land

Shore duty can be quite an adventure, taking you from the Pentagon in Washington, DC, to exciting locations throughout the world. Your assignments might be to naval facilities, air stations, technical schools, or command headquarters anywhere in the United States or overseas.

The skills and discipline learned in the Navy are assets wherever you go. Navy career fields such as construction, communications, and administration are important in the civilian workforce, too. The dedicated and highly qualified people ashore help keep the Navy's ships at sea. It's teamwork at its best.

Enlisting

To enlist you must be between seventeen and thirty-four years of age, and enlistments are for four, five, or six years, depending on which program you qualify for and choose. There are more than eighty job skills open to men and women, and you most likely would receive job training (after finishing basic training) at one of the many Navy schools. The more education you have, the better your job and pay, so be sure to at least finish high school. That all-important diploma is a requirement for entering many of the Navy's technical programs. Single and married men and women are eligible to join the Navy, but single parents with child custody are not.

You may enlist and delay reporting for active duty for up to twelve months, depending on the program you have selected. There is also a program that enables friends to take their recruit training together and/or be assigned together to their first duty station. Once accepted, you are a Navy enlistee and ready for your basic training.

Boot Camp

Boot camp takes place at one of the naval training centers. Officially, it has the more dignified title of Recruit Training Command or RTC. (Boot camp got its name years ago when the recruits wore leggings that looked like boots.) In the Navy, men and women train together, usually at the center nearest to their homes.

Receipt day is aptly named as the day of your arrival. It is the day you receive your introductory and processing instructions. You join other enlistees to form a company of about eighty members. You will stay with your new companions throughout boot camp. For the first day or two you will be busy filling out forms, obtaining clothing, and being indoctrinated. Each company has training instructors, called company commanders or CCs, who will be with you throughout your RTC and instruct you in everything you need to know about Navy protocol, day-to-day living, and Navy rules and regulations.

Ten formal training sessions are given each day. They embrace three subjects: administration and processing, military and naval training, and technical training. Some of the numerous subjects that you must master include accident prevention, basic seamanship, first aid, inspections, officer recognition, personal hygiene, security, security at sea, and time management.

In addition, you will find that great emphasis is placed on physical fitness, with plenty of calisthenics. By the time you graduate you will be running two miles at a time. Before you finish boot camp, you must pass certain physical fitness tests. Furthermore, it is natural for the Navy to insist on proficiency in water skills. You will be expected to demonstrate that you can enter water feet-first from a height of five feet and tread water or float for five minutes. You will swim fifty yards in the pool in five minutes, using any stroke, but keeping your head above the water. After instruction, you will have to show that you can use clothing or other buoyant objects to stay afloat.

In a typical RTC training day, you start at 5:30 A.M. After a hearty breakfast, you report for a four-hour training period followed by an hour and a half off for lunch. Another four-hour session is scheduled for the afternoon. After dinner the evening is spent taking care of personal matters, clothing, and equipment; cleaning the barracks; studying; and perhaps writing letters.

During RTC training you are granted no liberty and are permitted no visitors. Once graduation day arrives, however, your parents and friends are welcome to attend the ceremonies and dine with you in the dining room. During the graduation ceremony, when you pass in review, you will receive your set of orders; these orders will tell you where to report for your permanent base or your course of technical training. Now you will be granted leave for a few days, and you must take this leave before you arrive at your first duty station.

Upon completion of basic training, seamen go to technical schools, known as Class A schools, or are ordered to the fleet for duty and on-the-job training via a four-week apprenticeship course that enhances basic technical skills learned in recruit training. Enlisted recruits enter and complete boot camp as an E-1, but some recruits are promoted meritoriously to E-2. See the appendices for a list of typical career fields together with duties and responsibilities, qualifications, and examples of civilian jobs.

Promotion Requirements
- To seaman apprentice (E-2)—nine months active duty with commander's approval.

- To seaman (E-3)—nine months time in grade, demonstrated military and professional qualifications, and commander's approval.
- To petty officer third class (E-4) and above (up to E-9)— based on Navy-wide vacancies within each career field. (Note: Advancement to the more senior pay grades involves a selection board to determine who is best qualified.) Must also meet certain minimum time in grade requirements (which vary from six months to three years depending on the pay grade), be recommended for advancement by commander, complete education and training requirements, and compete on Navy-wide examinations.

Navy Life

"Navy life: it's not just a job, it's an adventure"; so says the U.S. Navy, and it points out some of the reasons for this statement in its publication, *Navy, What's in It for You?* These reasons include:

- Serving in the Navy is an exciting challenge. It can take you all over the world and expose you to new people, new places, and a new life.
- The Navy is a good place to work. It has the finest ships and aircraft and the most sophisticated equipment.
- Being an officer or an enlisted man or woman makes it possible to respond to the age-old call to "go down to the sea." It has caused men to sign up as sailors for generations.
- As a member of the naval establishment, you are able to obtain the finest training and education for the job ahead.

- Ability is the basis of advancement. Navy people are encouraged to use their abilities to the fullest to get ahead.

Shipboard Life at Sea

Your typical day aboard a ship will probably start at 6:00 A.M. You eat at 7:00 A.M., noon, and 5:00 P.M. These hours may be shifted somewhat depending on your schedule, since everyone cannot dine at the same time. At 8:00 A.M. you will attend the daily crew muster. Then you will work in four-hour periods. You may stand watch or perform whatever your specialized duty may be. Anticipate working as many as twelve hours a day. In case of an attack, you have a special battle station to which you report. You have another post in the event of some other kind of an emergency.

When off duty you may use the library, recreation and hobby rooms, and possibly see a movie every night. On Sunday you may want to attend a religious service. Remember that when at sea, no alcoholic beverages are permitted. As for your personal needs, on larger ships you will find a tailor, a shoe repair shop, laundry, and ship stores. On many ships there are doctors and dentists to care for your health.

If you have sea duty, you do not spend all your time at sea. The ship has a home port. It spends about six months a year in or near that port. The routine of being at sea is broken by frequent visits to other ports. Many of them are places you may always have wanted to see. As you travel, you are putting all your training and skills to the actual test. You are being given as much responsibility and challenge as you can handle.

Life Ashore

At your shore station, you will live either in traditional barracks or in one of the new enlisted living quarters that resemble college dormitories. Depending on the size of your station, you might find entertainment facilities such as recreation rooms with TV and stereo sets, pianos, and writing tables; a soda bar; a well-stocked library; and a base exchange store. First-run movies will probably be shown at discount prices.

Other leisure time activities might include participating in amateur theatricals, doing hobbies and crafts, or playing cards, chess, or checkers. You could also join a jazz band, shoot pool, and enjoy a variety of other activities. Most shore stations have clubs and lounges for enlisted personnel. There it is possible to relax, buy snacks and beverages, meet friends, and enjoy yourself. Every station is staffed with chaplains representing various faiths. You are encouraged to continue your religious activities while you are in the service.

Life in a Nuclear Submarine

The high-pitched klaxon sounds twice. Immediately you hear the warning over the loudspeakers: "Dive! Dive! Dive!"

Although the submarine is disappearing beneath the surface of the sea, you feel no sensation. Only the officer peering through the periscope and watching the waves closing over the boat is aware that the craft has begun its descent. In sixty seconds you have slipped down several hundred feet. Then the crew members at the controls send the sub forward, to cruise through the water at twenty miles an hour or better.

You are aboard a nuclear-powered attack submarine. It is one of some ninety in the Navy's fleet. You know that it might be sixty to eighty days before you surface again. Meanwhile, you will be busy working your watch as a trained sonar technician in the cramped sonar area with its subdued blue lighting. Here you and others wearing headphones sit before computer screens and watch the short twisting green lines and flashing orange numbers that tell you the sound frequencies coming from objects in the submarine's vicinity.

The sub's nose contains a large *sonar* (derived from the words *so*und, *na*vigation, and *r*anging). Sonar takes sound readings of the surrounding ocean and feeds back what it hears to the sonar operators. Special computers also receive the sounds. They select those that are characteristic of machinery or other mechanical noises. Sensitive devices analyze these sounds. They match them against sounds known to be emitted by foreign submarines. These sounds are stored in the computer's memory. Today fish, shrimp, and other marine life create most of the squiggles and other noises you see on your screen.

At the conclusion of your watch, you make your way to the enlisted personnel's mess area. There you can always obtain juices and ice cream. This is one of the few fairly open spaces in the sub. On some submarines its red vinyl booths and loud music create the illusion of a modern diner. Other recreational options include watching videotape movies, listening to the stereo, and visiting the library. If you are eager for a little exercise, you might jog in place in the engine room (where the temperature may be a comfortable eighty-five degrees), or you might do chin-ups in one of the narrow passageways.

At bedtime you find an unoccupied bunk. There are only ninety-four bunks for 134 sailors. Hence no one has the luxury of a private bedroom. The long narrow bunks are built three high with only curtains for privacy. You must fit all of your personal effects and clothing into a single drawer.

Food is up to Navy standard. Just before the sub leaves on its regular cruise, a ninety-day supply is stowed aboard. At first it is necessary to stack up cases in every nook and cranny. This ensures that there are ample provisions for the busy cooks who prepare three hearty meals a day plus midnight rations.

You and your shipmates have no sense of claustrophobia or boredom while confined in the huge steel tube for weeks at a time. There is a strong sense of community and pride in the job and the ship. There is the satisfaction of knowing you are part of a team effort that is so vital to the nation's security.

Your attack submarine has one crew of officers and men who stay with the ship. As a rule, you remain at sea as long as the crews of the larger ballistic missile subs do, but there the situation is different. Because of the strategic value of its weapons systems and longer patrols beneath the ocean's surface, the ballistic missile sub requires two separate crews, the blue and the gold. While one crew is ashore on leave and engaged in training, the other is aboard and on station. Some of these submarines are deployed from overseas sites, which is not true of attack subs. The crews must often be flown between their home port and the deployment site. Total time ashore between ballistic missile submarine patrols often amounts to eighty or ninety days.

The Flattop Miracle

Imagine an airport located near a large city. Ninety-five jet aircraft are based in its hangars and there are fifty-seven hundred employees, including pilots and maintenance crews. In addition, there are the control tower, repair shops, storage tanks for jet fuel, restaurants, a motel, recreational facilities, and storage space for all the food and other supplies.

Now place this airport on a ship at sea and you have an aircraft carrier. It is a tremendous vessel with its flattop, or flight deck, and aircraft hangars beneath it. This floating airport is complete in every way. It also stores ammunition and bombs needed for the aircraft as well as fuel required for the ship's engines if it is not nuclear powered. As one of the people aboard this floating airport, you are living and working in what might be described as an almost unbelievable world apart.

Careers as a Naval Officer

According to *Navy, What's in It for You?*, a career as an officer in the Navy can be described in this way:

> Navy officers are the leaders and managers of today's Navy. The Navy relies heavily on its officers. The corps of about fifty-four thousand men and women supplies the necessary leadership at every level of operations and management. It also provides the professional, scientific, and technical skills demanded by the wide variety of occupations found at sea and ashore. Every leadership position in the civilian world—executive, managerial, professional, scientific, and technical—probably has a counterpart in the Navy.
>
> In general, naval officer occupations fall into one of two major categories: operations and management, which includes executive and managerial positions with the fleet and the shore establishment; or scientific and technical, which includes all areas of professional expertise recognized in civilian life, such as medicine, health care specialties, engineering, scientific research, law, and religion.
>
> Navy officers must be college graduates. While those with technical majors are preferred, there are many opportunities for non-science majors. A system of regular job rotation and varied duty assignments, coupled with progressively advancing education and training, help ensure an officer's professional career development while in the Navy.

These two categories are further divided into unrestricted line, restricted line, and staff corps. Those who command the Navy's operating forces—that is, the ships, aircraft, submarines, operational fleets, and staffs—are the unrestricted line officers. The men and women who perform specialized duties in technical fields such as cryptology, aeronautical engineering, oceanography and hydrography, or ship engineering are known as restricted line officers. Finally, staff corps officers consist of those who have special responsibilities. They serve in such areas as supply, civil engineer, judge advocate general, medical, dental, or the chaplain corps.

Naval officers serve aboard aircraft carriers, cruisers, frigates, destroyers, and support ships. They also serve on attack and ballistic missile submarines. In modern aircraft they are Navy pilots and flight officers. And they serve on the shore in naval air stations, shipyards, electronics and ordnance laboratories, nuclear plants, supply depots, schools, communication stations, and other facilities.

The Navy places great reliance on its officers. The officers supply the leadership at every level of management and operations. The Navy tries to match your personal needs and preferences with the needs of the service. Professional development patterns are outlined in the Navy booklet *Officer Programs and Careers*.

As the Navy becomes a nuclear-powered service, more nuclear-trained naval officers are required. This field presents unusual opportunities for those who qualify. The goal of those who train for this specialty is supervisory responsibility for the maintenance and operation of ship and submarine nuclear power plants.

There are several roads to becoming a naval officer: the United States Naval Academy; Naval ROTC; Officer Candidate School; or by direct commission if you are trained in a profession such as medicine, law, engineering, or science. See Chapter 8 for more information about these opportunities.

For all the facts about the Navy, see your nearest recruiting officer, whose telephone number and address are listed in the phone book under United States Government, or write to Commander, Navy Recruiting Command, (Code 314), 801 North Randolph Street, Arlington, Virginia 22203-1991. You may also telephone for information at (800) USA-NAVY. Perhaps the best introduction is to tour the Navy via its highly informative website at http://www.navy.mil.

3

THE MARINE CORPS

From the halls of Montezuma
To the shores of Tripoli;
We fight our country's battles
In the air, on land, and sea;
First to fight for right and freedom
And to keep our honor clean;
We are proud to claim the title of
United States Marine.

So READS THE first verse of the famous *Marine Hymn*, a fitting introduction to our story of this venerable military service.

A Long History

On November 10, 1775, the Continental Congress adopted a resolution creating two battalions of Marines to serve as landing forces for the Continental Navy. Recruiting took place at Philadelphia's Tun Tavern, where owner Robert Mullan posted a notice offering new recruits an enticing mix of glory, adventure, ample food and drink—and a $17 cash enlistment bonus. Young men flocked to the tavern in droves and eagerly signed up to join the newly formed service. In 1776 the fledgling corps staged its first amphibious raid on foreign soil in the Bahamas. The Marines continued to fight throughout the course of the Revolutionary War. When the Treaty of Paris ended the war in 1783, both the Continental Navy and the Marines were disbanded.

Most of the Marines returned home. Then, when French and Barbary Coast pirates started attacking American commercial ships, the federal government moved swiftly to bring back the Marines. Congress reestablished the Corps on July 11, 1798. The service was attached to the Navy. Its mission would take place on both land and sea.

Over the years this original mission has remained virtually unchanged. Today, however, the Marine Corps—as symbolized by its trademark insignia combining a globe, an anchor, and an eagle—also conducts operations by air. The Marines continue to function under the Navy. The Marine Corps commandant reports directly to the secretary of the Navy and is also a member of the Joint Chiefs of Staff. The Marine Corps remains the smallest of our nation's four armed services; but its members share a unique esprit de corps that is rooted in a commendable history.

A Proud Tradition

After the Marines were reestablished in 1798, they fought hard and well in France and in Santo Domingo. In 1804 a handful of Marines joined a disparate band of Arab horsemen and mercenaries and marched some five hundred miles across North Africa to capture the port town of Derna, which was being controlled by a corrupt potentate who supported piracy. The Marines helped pull down the enemy flag and raised the Stars and Stripes over "the shores of Tripoli." Marines were active in most of the engagements of the War of 1812 and again in the war with Mexico. This time they distinguished themselves by capturing Vera Cruz and Mexico City. There they led the way to Mexico's national palace, the "halls of Montezuma." These acts later were memorialized in the Marine's hymn, in the lines "From the halls of Montezuma to the shores of Tripoli." Subsequently the Marines have distinguished themselves in operations too numerous to include in added verses of their hallowed hymn.

During the 1920s there was a rash of mail robberies in the United States. Marines were dispatched to watch over the U.S. mail. A year before the country entered World War II, Marines were serving in China, the Philippines, the Hawaiian Islands, Guam, the Panama Canal Zone, and at Guantanamo Bay, Cuba. Several thousand other Marines stood guard at munitions plants, ammunition depots, and Navy yards. Some four thousand were on board Navy ships. Although the Corps was involved in numerous invasions during World War II, it is best remembered for its role in the capture of Iwo Jima and the stirring picture of the three Marines planting the American flag atop Mount Suribachi.

On October 23, 1983, the Marine Corps experienced what was probably its greatest tragedy. While helping to keep the peace in war-torn Lebanon, Marines were living in their headquarters building in the city of Beirut. Early that morning, a sentry guarding the building was unable to stop a terrorist who drove a truck past him into the yard. Within seconds the driver detonated some twelve thousand pounds of explosives that immediately destroyed the high-rise and killed 237 sleeping Marines. Within a few months orders came to withdraw all Marines from Beirut, and doubtless many of those leaving reflected on the fruitless and tragic cost of this mission—a mission like every other assignment that had to be carried out.

What Are Marines?

The Marines call themselves "the few and the proud." They make absolutely no bones about the fact that they are tough and disciplined. They proudly state that they willingly face extreme mental and physical challenges of any kind. The Marine Corps describes its members as follows: "He or she will be physically fit and strong, and will be able to adapt. This is the basic Marine warrior, and it's the blueprint that every Marine builds from." The Marines attract new recruits by issuing a challenge: "Transform your body. Sharpen your mind. Crush your limitations." They acknowledge one another with their favorite saying: *semper fidelis*, which means "always faithful."

Marines are expected to be quick thinking and hard working and to be an ally in any situation. The Pentagon classifies them as expeditionary troops, based at sea but able to operate from the air or on land to stabilize or contain international disturbance. One look at a Marine in uniform—the way he or she carries him or herself with confidence and pride—confirms that these special troops place a high value on discipline and comportment.

The Corps maintains a strong martial arts program. Described by the Corps as imparting "equal parts agility, discipline, and character," this program teaches Marines ". . . how to disarm and subdue enemies without necessarily having to use deadly force."

Organization of the Marine Corps

The Marine Corps operates as a separate service within the Department of the Navy, and its commandant is a full member of the Joint Chiefs of Staff. As of late 2004, the Marines were the smallest of the services in terms of personnel, with 177,480 people on active duty. From an organizational point of view, it comprises two principal sections: the operating forces and the supporting establishment.

The Marines' top priority is combat readiness. Their traditional peacetime role is to serve as a force-in-readiness. The Corps has a global outlook; Marines are ready to be sent anywhere on immediate notice to carry out missions. The Marines emphasize physical fitness and intensive training. Thus they are ready for emergencies. They have a tradition of being on the alert and ready at all times. Consequently, they maintain three rapid-response air-ground task forces, elements of which are continuously deployed in the Mediterranean Sea, the western Pacific Ocean, and the Indian Ocean.

Do these far-flung operations of the Marines interest you? Have you always wanted to travel and live in exotic places overseas? The Marines have much to offer in the way of careers that offer the possibility of travel.

The Enlisted Marine

Signing up for the Marine Corps starts by contacting the nearest Marine recruiting office. If none is listed in your telephone book under United States Government, contact USMC, P.O. Box 2360, Chatsworth, California 91313-9779, or www.marines.com.

Testing and other preparation for entering the Corps is similar to that conducted by the other services. The Marine enlistment-options program lets you choose an assignment in a field where your interests lie even before you enlist. If you are qualified, you could train in one of thirty-five occupational fields.

As with all the services, once you are in the Marine Corps you go for your basic training. The Corps has little to say about this phase of your training except: "It all starts in boot camp. That's what being part of a proud military tradition demands—physically, mentally, and emotionally." Basic training has already been described in the section on the Navy. Although the Marine boot camp program has had a reputation for being anything but pleasant, remember that most enlistees get through it satisfactorily. Otherwise, there would be no Marine Corps.

There is no typical day during boot camp; however, to give you some idea of the general framework, here is a rough schedule:

- At 6:00 A.M. reveille sounds. You rise, wash, make your bed, and may have light physical exercise or training, followed by breakfast and then a "police call" to clean your quarters and around the barracks.
- At 8:00 A.M. the flag is hoisted and the band plays the national anthem. The balance of the morning may be devoted to drills, inspections, and other programs.
- At 11:30 A.M. dinner is served.
- At 1:00 P.M. until finishing time there are more drills, training, and perhaps other programs.
- At 5:00 P.M. supper is served, followed by free time unless training or other programs are scheduled.
- At 10:00 P.M. is bedtime.

If you honestly question your desire or ability to stand the discipline and rigorous physical training necessary to complete boot camp successfully, you may not be psychologically or physically ready to be a Marine. Don't jump to conclusions though. Get all the facts first. Talk with the Marine recruiter, who can help and advise you. Be fair to yourself and to the Marine Corps.

Career Opportunities

Undoubtedly the average American has a mental image of a Marine as a good looking, rugged soldier who is either wading ashore under gunfire, fighting in a dense jungle, or raising the American flag on the peak of a hill following a deadly battle.

There is no question about the infantryman—be he a rifleman, machine gunner, or mortarman—being the "guts" of the outfit, for he (women are excluded so far from combat duty) is the one who does much of the actual fighting and winning, whatever the military objective. Nevertheless, the Corps must have other men and women to provide the infantry with everything it needs. As is the case with all of the services, a wide range of specialists is required for a variety of essential jobs both in the field and in the shops or offices.

One way to obtain a flavor of Marine Corps jobs is to sample the courses open to enlisted Marines. Here is what the Marine Corps says about education: "It is the Marine Corps' attitude that a better educated Marine is a better Marine. It is the expressed philosophy of the Corps that no Marines should have the opportunity for education foreclosed just because they didn't get it before they enlisted."

The following course titles provide only a portion of the education the Marine Corps offers to its enlisted personnel. The school locations are included.

Course Title and School Location
Amphibious Warfare School—Quantico, VA
Assault Amphibian School—Camp Pendleton, CA
Combat Water Survival Swimming School—Quantico, VA
Defense Information School—Ft. Meade, MD
Enlisted Professional Military Education—Quantico, VA
Expeditionary Warfare Training—Sites in CA and VA
Financial Management School—Camp Lejeune, NC
Firefighting School—Goodfellow AFB, TX
Infantry School—Camp Pendleton, CA; Camp Lejeune, NC
Instructional Management School—Camp Lejeune, NC
Intelligence School—Dam Neck, VA
Landing Signals Officers Course—Naval Air Station, VA
Logistics Instruction School—Quantico, VA
Mountain Warfare Training—Bridgeport, CA
NCO Academy—Quantico, VA
Officer Candidate School—Quantico, VA
Personnel and Legal Services School—Camp Lejeune, NC
Senior NCO Academy—Quantico, VA
Supply School—Camp Lejeune, NC
Survival, Resistance, Evasion, & Escape—North Island, CA

Opportunities for Musicians, Too!

Music has been a tradition in the Marines from the very beginning, when drummers and fifers were enlisted in the first and second battalions of the original Continental Marines, which were authorized by Congress in 1775. Then, in 1798, President John Adams established the United States Marine Band as an aid in enticing young recruits to join the Corps. Three years later the band played for President Jefferson's inaugural. The Marine Band has performed at every inaugural celebration since that time. It is interesting to note that the world-famous John Philip Sousa directed the band from 1880 until 1892.

You will find a Marine Band in a variety of settings. The musicians perform in concerts that vary from traditional military ceremonies to combo performances for officially hosted receptions. The Marine Band appears in Tournament of Roses, Cotton Bowl, and Mardi Gras parades. You can hear the band at Independence Day and Armed Forces Day celebrations, to say nothing of popular sporting events. Smaller ensembles often perform for recruiting and community-related events.

If this branch of the service interests you, you must be qualified for regular enlistment, pass a musical audition, and successfully complete Marine Corps Recruit Training (boot camp). If you have unusual talent, here is an opportunity worth investigating.

Promotion Requirements

Advancement is determined by the manner Marines perform their duties and demonstrate leadership potential. The top 10 percent of privates graduating from basic training may be meritoriously promoted by their commanding general. For military pay chart information, see Chapter 7.

- To private 1st class (E-2)—six months active duty.
- To lance corporal (E-3)—eight months time in grade and nine months time in service.
- To corporal (E-4)—eight months time in grade and twelve months time in service.
- To sergeant (E-5)—twelve months time in grade and twenty-four months time in service.

- To staff sergeant and above (E-6 through E-9)—various time in grade requirements are based on the needs of the Marine Corps.

Special Field Training

In addition to the courses listed here, you may find several special courses that prepare you for the following duties that are somewhat out of the ordinary.

- **Sea duty.** This involves serving on board ship with a Marine detachment.
- **Embassy duty.** This involves guarding and providing security for more than one hundred United States embassies, consulates, and legations throughout the world.
- **Barracks duty.** This involves many cities and countries throughout the world. One example is the famous Marine Barracks in Washington, DC. Marines are assigned to this facility to help guard the president of the United States and to provide honor guards for state functions and other special occasions.
- **Inspector-instructor duty.** This involves helping run units of the Marine Corps Reserve and taking care of administrative details.
- **Recruiting duty.** This involves becoming the Corps' representative in the community as an information specialist and career counselor. It also involves meeting with and advising those who are interested in learning about the Corps.

- **Drill instructor duty.** This involves being in a position of leadership as a drill instructor. Drill instructors shape the future of the Corps by training all of its new recruits.

Preparation for these careers requires varying lengths of time. Courses are usually given at San Diego, California; Parris Island, South Carolina; and Quantico, Virginia.

To be eligible to join the Marine Corps as an enlisted man or woman, you should be between seventeen and twenty-eight years old and a United States citizen. You must be able to pass the physical examination and be of good moral character.

The Marine Corps believes that the more education you have, the better a Marine you will be. The Corps wants you to finish high school before becoming a Marine, but if you don't have your high school diploma or a recognized equivalent, your Marine recruiter will explain the ways that the Corps will help you get it. Some young recruits, for example, obtain a diploma by taking the GED (General Education Diploma) test.

If you qualify, you will be guaranteed training in one of the Marine option programs. You choose the occupational area most desirable to you, and the Marines make the guarantee before you enlist. The guarantee is in the form of a written contract that requires on your part a four-, five-, or six-year enlistment, depending on the option program you choose.

Officers in the Marines

The first statement in the Marine Corps booklet says this about opportunities for officers:

The relation between officers and men should in no sense be that of superior and inferior, that of master and servant, but rather that of teacher and scholar. In fact, it would partake of the nature of the relationship between father and son to the extent that officers . . . are responsible for the physical, mental, and moral welfare as well as the discipline and military training of the young men under their command.

Regardless of the program you have entered to train for an officer's commission, you will attend the Officers Candidate School at Quantico, Virginia. All commissioning programs require that you have at least a bachelor's degree. At Quantico you will experience weeks of some of the hardest physical training in the world. You will negotiate an obstacle course you never thought you could handle. You will learn to take and give commands, tell the difference between tactical and nontactical marches, and identify every tiny detail of your rifle and pistol. You will become proficient in concealment and camouflage, combat signals and formations, and the operations of fire teams in defensive and offensive positions. The emphasis will be on leadership whether you are female or male. You will also be given temporary leadership positions, so your appearance, speech, command presence, strength, agility, coordination, endurance, and intelligence, as well as your moral and physical courage can be evaluated. Most important of all, you must be able to lead other Marines under conditions of extreme stress.

Actually you will be evaluated in two areas. They are:

- **Graded events.** Your military knowledge and skills are measured by written examinations and practical application in land navigation, technique of military instruction, rifle and pistol qualification, and the physical fitness test.
- **Leadership.** Leadership evaluation is conducted by means of two command evaluations and a written exam. You are

measured by your instructors in terms of acceptance of responsibility, attention to duty, use of authority, attitude, judgment, common sense, cooperation, initiative, and command presence.

This evaluation is just the beginning. Every career officer, either ground or aviation, can reasonably expect to participate in five basic forms of duty: student instructor of other Marines, command of tactical units, special assignments like sea duty, naval attaché or recruiting, and staff assignment with major Marine units or other services.

Here is what can happen if you make a career in the Corps. During your first five or six years, you will be trained in an occupational field and obtain varied experience with promotion to first lieutenant and perhaps be selected for captain. During the next five or six years, you will have additional professional training as an officer with an assignment as a commanding officer of a company or executive officer of a battalion or squadron. You are being groomed for better jobs ahead.

By the time of your twenty-first or twenty-second year, you will be a lieutenant colonel—a headquarters staff officer, an inspector-instructor in a Marine reserve unit, or a member of a joint service staff. During the rest of your career you might be a colonel or general. Now you are a top-level executive, a policy- and decision-maker, a leader of men and women at the peak of your career: an officer of the Marine Corps.

Are the Marines for You?

To assess your aptitude and eligibility for entering the Marine Corps, it might help to ask yourself these questions:

- Does the prospect of becoming a Marine officer appeal to you?
- Are you eager to train as a pilot or flight officer?
- Are you looking for money for college?
- Do you prefer a full-time civilian career combined with the excitement of a part-time opportunity in the Marine Reserve and the chance to attend college?
- Is there anything else you would like to learn about how you might fit into the Marine Corps?

If you've answered yes to some of these questions, contact the nearest Marine recruitment office, which is listed in most telephone books under United States Government. Or write: USMC, P.O. Box 2360, Chatsworth, California 91313-9779. You can also check the Marine Corps' website at http://www.usmc.mil.

4

THE ARMY

You're in the Army now,
You're not behind the plow.
You'll never get rich
Diggin' a ditch
You're in the Army now.

DOUBTLESS YOU'VE HEARD this old ditty that has been handed down from generation to generation from the time when soldiers dug trenches for various purposes, including protection. Today those verses no longer apply. Most recruits don't come from farms. And although they still don't hope to get rich in the Army, service members reap rewards from pay and benefits, from serving their country, and from the knowledge that Army training is excellent preparation for a lucrative civilian job.

Dwight Eisenhower—General and President

When young Dwight was almost two years old, his family moved to Abilene, Kansas, where his father found a job in a creamery. The family was poor, and there were six growing boys to feed. Dwight's mother tended fruits and vegetables in the backyard and sold whatever produce the family did not need. When Dwight was in high school, he worked nights at the creamery to provide extra income for his family. After graduation he took a full-time job there so he could help his brother Edgar, who was a freshman at the University of Michigan.

Someone suggested to Dwight that he try for an appointment to the Naval Academy at Annapolis or to the Military Academy at West Point. Too old for Annapolis, Dwight received an appointment to West Point, which he entered in 1911. After graduation he rose steadily through the Army ranks. During World War II he became the supreme commander of the Allied Expeditionary Forces and was in charge of the massive invasion of Europe in June 1944. After the war, Dwight served as president of Columbia University until President Truman asked him to once again wear the uniform, this time as supreme commander for the Allied Powers in Europe, the military force for the North Atlantic Treaty Organization. The rest is history. In 1952 Americans went to the polls and elected Dwight D. Eisenhower the thirty-fourth president of the United States.

Dwight Eisenhower was not the only member of the United States Army to become president. George Washington, who was commander of the Continental Army during the Revolutionary War, became our first president. He was followed by others with military backgrounds: James Madison, Andrew Jackson, William Harrison,

Zachary Taylor, Ulysses S. Grant, Rutherford Hayes, James Garfield, Benjamin Harrison, William McKinley, Theodore Roosevelt, and Harry Truman. If you choose to enter the Army, you might not become president, but you will have the opportunity to find a satisfying and rewarding career in the service.

Evolution of Armies

Historically, armies date back at least as far as 3200 B.C., when the Babylonians had a regular standing army of bowmen and spearmen. About seven hundred years later (2500 B.C.), the Sumerians introduced the first chariots in battles. Another major development occurred about 55 B.C. At this time the Greeks devised the phalanx, eight rows of heavily armed spearmen who formed a solid rectangle. Although a phalanx could not move quickly, it did withstand a cavalry charge. Next, the Romans organized their numerous legions of soldiers, many of whom were superb technicians, forerunners of our modern Army with its Corps of Engineers. They established an empire throughout Europe and Great Britain and built excellent roads, bridges, walls, and forts, the remains of which may be seen in many places.

The introduction of gunpowder revolutionized warfare. By the late 1600s, soldiers who carried muskets could defend themselves against charging cavalry as well as enemy infantry. The Industrial Revolution during the first half of the 1800s made it possible to mass-produce better guns and other armaments. Later, the inventions of the automobile and airplane gave rise to a whole new concept of warfare with tanks, motorized vehicles, and planes. In World War I, the infantry fought mostly in muddy trenches, but when World War II broke out in 1939, soldiers saw fewer trenches and not as many long marches. More tanks and other motorized equipment were employed, while airplanes quickly moved paratroops and other soldiers hundreds of miles to new fronts. Victory depended also on the factory worker at home, who built up the "arsenal of democracy." These workers produced a never-ending stream of tanks, jeeps, trucks, planes, guns, and other implements of war that were necessary to the military campaigns of the mid-twentieth century.

When the first atomic bomb was exploded in Japan in 1945, a new kind of destructive weapon was added—a weapon so terrible that in subsequent years no other such bombs have been used. Fear of nuclear devastation has compelled armies to continue to fight with pre-atomic weapons of artillery, tanks, planes, and surprise attacks on the enemy. However, newer weapons are being forged around lasers and other advanced scientific discoveries.

The United States Army

The United States Army is the oldest branch of the armed services. It was founded on June 14, 1775, by the Continental Congress. That was when the Army consisted of foot soldiers who had to walk or march wherever they went. These soldiers depended on their muzzle-loading muskets for protection and attack and had only horses and lumbering wagons to transport their ammunition and supplies. Today the soldier has evolved considerably. For one thing, he is no longer necessarily a he. A soldier is just as likely to be a female as a male. The soldier no longer embarks on long, forced marches (except under exceptional circumstances). Now he or she rides. Instead of pouring powder and a single bullet into the muzzle of a gun, the soldier carries an automatic gun capable of firing a barrage of bullets at the touch of the trigger. Instead of having to rely on spies to search for enemy positions, the soldier uses modern communications to locate distant targets and fire at them with great accuracy.

Army Organization

The Army is the largest of the nation's armed services. It has nearly five hundred thousand men and women in the active Army and many more in the Reserves. This does not include the thousands of civilians who can be considered part of the Army team.

The active Army includes eleven major commands, each of which is served by an assortment of numbered armies, corps, divisions, brigades, and battalions. Although all soldiers fall under one of the major commands—for instance, U.S. Army Europe, U.S. Army Pacific, or Special Operations Command—the soldiers' functions generally are governed through the divisions. Soldiers will go to war, for instance, along with others in their division. In war or in peace, a division might be compared to a good-sized town. It requires most of the same types of workers a town might need: administrative personnel, police officers, computer operators, cooks, finance and legal clerks, journalists, mechanics, radar technicians—and warriors.

Here are the most common levels of command in the Army.

- **Division.** 10,000–17,000 people, commanded by a major general
- **Brigade.** 2,000–4,000 people, commanded by a colonel (There are usually three brigades in a division.)
- **Battalion.** 500–1,000 people, commanded by a lieutenant colonel
- **Company.** 100–200 people, commanded by a captain
- **Platoon.** 30–50 people, usually led by a lieutenant
- **Squad.** 5–10 people, led by a staff sergeant or a sergeant

Army Personnel

The great majority of men and women serving in the Army are enlisted members, most of whom sign up after graduation from high school. Once in the service, there is opportunity to advance through the ranks from private to sergeant major. You might even become a commissioned officer if you have the necessary qualifications and complete the advanced and specialized training.

There are three ways you can become a commissioned officer in the Army:

1. By attending the West Point Military Academy (see Chapter 8).
2. By attending Officer Candidate School (see Chapter 8).
3. By direct appointment if you are professionally qualified as a chaplain, civil engineer, lawyer, or in a medical or allied health service field. Some of these positions are mentioned later in this chapter.

You may also work for the Army as a civilian employee under the federal Civil Service as explained in this chapter.

Enlisting

There are several requirements that you must meet before you are eligible to enlist in the Army.

- **Age.** Applicants must be between the ages of seventeen and thirty-five. Verification of age is required, such as a birth certificate or statement from the State Registrar of Vital Statistics, from other similar state officials, or from information recorded in official records. If no such record is available, you may submit a baptismal record or certified copy or a sworn statement by one or both parents or your legal guardian.

- **Citizenship.** Applicants must be citizens of the United States or aliens who have been lawfully admitted to the country for permanent residence.
- **Testing.** Qualifying scores are required on test batteries and, in some cases, subtests of the batteries. The test now in use is the ASVAB (Armed Services Vocational Aptitude Battery).
- **Education.** The Army prefers to enlist high school graduates. However, in some circumstances, non–high school graduates may be accepted. Your local Army recruiter can give you more information.
- **Medical fitness.** Enlistment standards can be explained by your Army recruiter. Some enlistment options call for special qualifications.
- **Other criteria.** Other important criteria include good character qualifications, police clearance, and moral screening.
- **Enlistment periods.** These vary from two to six years subject to certain exceptions. Some special programs may call for specific enlistment periods. Your local Army recruiter can give you the latest information.

Visiting the Army Recruiter

Let us assume you are interested in joining the Army—or at least in investigating the possibility. The first step is to contact the nearest Army recruiter. You will find the address in your telephone directory under U.S. Government—Army. If you cannot locate a listing, write to Headquarters, U.S. Army Recruiting Command, Fort Knox, Kentucky 40121-2726 or visit the Army's website at http://www.army.mil, and click on the link for recruiting.

The recruiter will meet you in the recruiting office, at your home, or possibly at school or work. The first interview is your chance to ask whatever questions you may have about the Army. The recruiter will want to learn about you, too—your interests, education, hobbies, goals, and your health. You should have the following documents ready: birth certificate, high school diploma or transcript documenting your midterm graduation or GED documentation, Social Security card, and letter from your doctor if you have (or had) any special medical condition that will require explanation during your Army physical examination.

The next step will be for the recruiter to make arrangements for you to take an aptitude test and a physical examination. This will be at no expense to you. In some areas the aptitude test may be given at a location near the recruiting station called an MET (mobile examining team) site. You can either take your physical immediately after the aptitude test or wait until you hear the results of the test before scheduling the physical. In either case the physical examination can only be done at the MEPS (military enlistment processing station) nearest your home. If necessary, meals and overnight lodging will be provided for you at a place near the MEPS—again at no expense to you.

Be prepared for a busy day, which will normally start about 7:00 A.M. First you will be told what you can expect to do during your visit; then you will have an opportunity to ask questions; finally you will be ready to start your processing. This is divided into three areas: mental (unless you were previously tested), medical, and administrative.

The mental test usually requires about two and a half hours to complete. You will want to do your best on this examination because the results will have considerable bearing on your selection of options before you enter the Army. Get a good night's sleep and eat a healthy breakfast; these will help you concentrate so you get good test scores.

Next comes the medical examination performed by medical doctors and trained technicians. Women are examined separately and in privacy, and a female escort is always present. The physical examination takes about two hours, after which you will have a conference with a doctor and discuss any problems that may have been discovered.

Your administrative processing comes after you have had an opportunity to talk with your Army guidance counselor, who may be female or male. He or she will take your mental test scores and physical evaluation and all the other information the Army has learned about you, feed the data into a small computer programmed to analyze the data, and then make suggestions that match your qualifications to the Army's needs.

Whether you decide to enlist and leave for active duty or join the DEP (Delayed Entry Program), a written agreement will be prepared setting out all the conditions of your enlistment, which you will be asked to review carefully with your guidance counselor. Should you sign up for the DEP, you have a year before you must leave on active duty.

Whether you have decided to enter the service immediately or have taken the DEP option, the first day arrives when you leave for your initial entry training. At the end of your bus, train, or plane ride you will arrive at the Army reception station—and you then know that "You're in the Army now."

Your First Days in the Army

During your short stay at the reception station, usually three working days, you live in barracks and are supervised by reception station personnel. While there you will go through the following processing procedures:

- You will receive your uniforms.
- Your personnel records will be processed.
- You will receive your identification card (ID).
- You will receive your immunization shots.
- You will have eye and dental checks.
- You will be given mental tests.
- Men will visit the barbershop for a haircut.

Later you will attend an orientation session. You will learn about medical and recreational facilities, religious activities, leave and pass policies, post exchange, legal assistance, various types of care available for your dependents, pay and allowances, service obligations, and other matters of concern to new enlistees. In between these activities you will attend classes in the barracks. You also will exercise, march, and take other short courses designed to help you adjust to Army living.

Now that you have had your indoctrination into the service, you are ready for basic training. Over the years, so many inaccurate rumors and frightening stories have circulated about this part of Army life that we asked the Army if we might include its own description of basic training in this book.

The information in the following section is taken from the booklet *You and the Army*. It will give you a good idea of what to expect during your first two months in the service.

Basic Training

You've learned a lot during your three days at the Reception Station. Now you're going to learn even more about the Army and yourself.

Basic training consists of a variety of activities including physical readiness training. This involves running, calisthenics, obstacle course, and so forth. Men and women receive essentially the same initial training, including weapons instruction, but they are trained separately.

By regulation, women cannot be assigned to combat or direct combat support units. But the Army believes that no matter what their specialty, soldiers should learn the basic combat skills that will give them the confidence and ability to defend themselves.

Both men and women can expect indoor and outdoor classes covering the following subjects: military courtesies and customs, drill and ceremonies, ID and wear of the uniform, inspections, guard duty, role of the Army, responsibility of a soldier, code of conduct, Geneva and Hague conventions, marches and bivouacs, basic rifle marksmanship, hand grenades, familiarization with U.S. weapons, personal affairs (service benefits), military justice, equal opportunity, hazards of drug and alcohol abuse, personal health and hygiene, individual protective measures for nuclear/biological/chemical defense, first aid, field hygiene and sanitation, individual tactical training techniques, fire and maneuver, defensive training, self-confidence.

Will it be tough? You bet it will. Someone figured out that you'll march more than 100 miles during your training. But if you're in reasonably good shape, the physical part of your training will be easier. But not too easy. If you did well in school, your classroom instruction will be easier. But not too easy. You'll use your muscles and your mind as you've never used them before. You'll be tired, sore, dusty, and a bit frayed around the edges at the end of each day. But if you try hard, you'll make it. A remarkably high percentage of the young people who come into the Army do.

Your Sergeant

The sergeant is the primary individual responsible for your training during this period. You'll probably think that this individual does an unusual amount of shouting, all of which seems directed at you.

But if it's any comfort, everyone in your training company feels the same way. So don't let it get to you. You're not being hassled or harassed. The sergeant's job is to turn you into a good soldier within a few short weeks. The shouting and toughness are all part of the process. You'll come to remember your sergeant, if not with affection, certainly with respect.

The weeks of basic training are filled with training challenges and experiences you will never forget. Some of the highlights you can expect follow below. (Note: The sequence of events may vary slightly at different posts, but the content will be generally the same everywhere.)

First Week

Your training starts out at a fast pace, but one you can handle. You do various exercises and running, called PT (physical training). You learn marching and facing movements and start on the Manual of Arms with your new-found buddy, the M-16 rifle. You'll study the functioning of this weapon, how to adjust sights, disassemble, and assemble. A drill sergeant will show you how to prepare for your first barracks inspection. And you'll learn that your first inspections are never good enough, but you'll get better.

During this week, you will also find yourself feeling better, despite sore muscles and a few aches. More PT—grass drills, various exercises, wind sprints, and running. You'll be introduced to the obstacle course. Tough stuff, but it's great for building confidence. You'll take a PT test to see how far you've come. One thing you'll realize: You couldn't have done it a week earlier. The week will end with a preparation for a foot and wall locker inspection, including field equipment and clothing.

Second Week

Most of this week will be spent on the firing range learning more about your M-16 rifle. You will receive lectures on firing range procedures, coaching, steady hold factors, and use of score cards. You'll also learn about sight adjustment, aiming point, and engaging surprise targets. There will be more PT. Another inspection comes up, too, this time in formation without your weapon.

Third Week

Most of this week will also be spent on the firing range practicing with your M-16 rifle. You will learn to fire from all positions, rapid reloading, and moving with a loaded weapon. You will also fire for record. Maybe you'll earn the badge of Marksman, Sharpshooter, or Expert. You will make tactical daylight marches and bivouacs. And just to keep you on your toes, a PT test and weapons inspection.

You'll be tired, and your muscles will be sore, but somehow you'll feel better all over. The week ends with the inevitable inspection. This time it is in formation with your weapon.

Fourth Week

You will be outdoors all week and will experience night training. You'll also be introduced to grenades and how to use them. Big stuff—you'll follow instructions very carefully. You also learn individual tactical techniques. And PT gets tougher—longer runs, road marches, obstacle course, the works. You'll get another test on what you've learned over the past week and, of course, another inspection.

Fifth Week

More night training, patrol, and bivouac security. You will receive instruction in first aid and a general review of PT and physical contact training exercises. You will learn that you don't dislike C-rations as much as you thought. The inspection this week consists of a field display on your bed in the barracks, foot and wall lockers, and in formation with your weapon.

Sixth Week

More tactical training, again mostly outdoors. You'll learn about additional weapons such as antipersonnel mines, antitank weapons, and grenade launchers. The interesting art of camouflage and its application on the battlefield will be taught and tested. All the while, you'll continue to become closer to your individual weapon, the M-16 rifle.

Seventh Week

All the pieces are starting to come together. That tactical training, PT, M-16 rifle practice and drill are all working for you. And while you're using camouflage to make yourself invisible, you'll be learning to recognize enemy personnel and equipment, both up close and at a distance. Soon you'll be able to identify terrain from the way it looks on a map, and find the best way to get across it.

And just so you don't forget, there's more PT, drill, and another inspection.

Eighth Week

Are you the same person who signed the enlistment agreement? You're not. You'll be tougher, more disciplined. Tired, maybe, but you seem to bounce back faster each day. During this week, you will review all you have learned and will be tested on it. Combat proficiency, physical conditioning, and basic military knowledge. You'll wonder how you've learned so much in a few short weeks.

This is the wrap-up. All training and tests are completed. At the end of the week, you'll take part in the graduation exercises and pass in review before the commander. You've made it. You are now a well-trained full-fledged soldier in the United States Army. It's been tough—but you've met the challenge.

Combat Soldiers

Before we tell you about the skill training programs in the myriad career fields, let's briefly consider the combat soldier and the positions available to those who want to enter this frontline field.

Infantry

This is the backbone of the Army. The Army is, in fact, defined by the infantry mission, around which the entire service revolves. As an infantryman, you will be in a position to carry out some of the nation's most vital—and dangerous—assignments. As an infantryman, you move on foot or via armored personnel carrier or helicopter. You move silently, by squads, slipping through the night, or you come running out shouting a battle cry. Your weapons are the finest and your training the best. This is where you will meet the greatest challenge of all: yourself.

Armor

An armor soldier is a direct descendant of the horse soldier, but with a 57-ton, 750-horsepower steel tank instead of a horse. The machine is an extension of you. As a gunner, a loader, or a driver, you get to know your machine as your skill and courage turn the rumbling giant into a fearful fighting machine.

Artillery

Here are the light artillery pieces, the huge guns, and the missiles that move into position on treads. Computers plot distance and trajectory while the gun crew, working together as one, responds to the target information. Technical skill and teamwork are the keys to success here.

Air Defense Artillery

In this branch of the service you may carry a small missile yourself and fire it, or help fire others that are so large that they require a launch team of thirty people. The responsibility here is to protect the Army's ground forces and, when necessary, civilian population centers from air attack. Soldiers in air defense artillery are trained in technical proficiency: radar operations and maintenance, communications, gunnery, missiles, fire control, and tracking. You will be a new kind of soldier with new kinds of weapons.

Combat Engineers

These engineers pave the way for advancing infantry and armor. They harass the foe with minefields, obstacles, and the precision destruction of bridge spans. In addition they build roads, bridges, gun emplacements, and airfields. Equally skilled with tools and weapons, the engineer is a vital part of the combat team, always ready to drop a tool and grab a rifle if the work is threatened. It calls for an individual who likes to work side by side with others of similar characteristics, overcoming obstacles and solving problems.

Airborne

The paratroopers are special soldiers who parachute to their fighting position from aircraft. Weeks of demanding airborne training must be completed before you are ready to make your first jump.

Rangers

These are the "go-anywhere" soldiers, the best-trained, most highly disciplined troops in the Army. If you volunteer for this branch, you must agree to live by a creed of honor and dedication that reads in part: "Surrender is not a Ranger word. I will never leave a fallen comrade to fall into the hands of the enemy, and under no circumstances will I ever embarrass my country." As a Ranger, you learn to survive and function under the most extreme conditions. You act as the eyes of the Army, probe deeply into unfriendly territory, and lead others on long-range reconnaissance missions—all because you have met the challenge of the toughest training the Army has to offer.

Special Forces

The most honored and respected fighting soldiers are individuals possessing many skills—a unique combination of Ranger and paratrooper, fighter and teacher. They are of the best physical and mental caliber, ready to serve anywhere, any time, through snow, jungle growth, over mountains, or dropped from the sky. These soldiers are specialists in communications, operation and intelligence, demolitions, weapons, or medicine, and they are cross-trained in other areas to double their usefulness. Only the brightest and the best are chosen to wear the proud emblem of the Special Forces—the Green Beret.

Now for the career training opportunities that will prepare you for one of the many combat or noncombat jobs, every one of which is vital to the Army's mission.

Career Options in the Army

You have completed your initial entry training; you should now have new confidence in yourself and what you can do as well as new physical and mental abilities. The next step is skill training.

What you do depends on the branch of the Army you have chosen or to which you have been assigned. It may consist of advanced training in one of the combat arms—infantry, armor, field or air defense artillery, or combat engineers—or perhaps on-the-job training or education at an Army service school. This part of your training will develop you for one of the hundreds of MOS (military occupational specialties) offered by the Army.

Skill training programs generally last from seven to nine weeks; some of the more technical can last for as many as forty weeks. Your training program will employ the most modern teaching methods available. It will combine practical, hands-on training on real equipment with expert classroom instruction. You will find the latest in teaching aids that will enable you to pace your own training and speed up your progress. The quality of training you receive could be difficult to match in civilian life at any price.

The Army is not just the infantry, nor is it a collection of individuals in uniform waiting for something to happen. The Army is a vast organization of men and women who have been educated and trained to do their best in their assigned occupational specialties. These specialties cover a wide range of job types, including administration, air defense artillery, air defense missile maintenance, aircraft maintenance, ammunition, and armor. There are also jobs such as automatic data processing, aviation communications-electronics systems maintenance, ballistic land-combat missile and light air-defense weapons-system maintenance, band member, and chemical technician. Other jobs are combat engineering, electronic warfare/cryptological operations, or electronic warfare/intercept systems maintenance. Then there are specialties in food service, law enforcement, and military intelligence. Many jobs are also available in public affairs and related fields, as well as in recruitment and reenlistment, supply, and transportation.

You may recall that before being accepted for enlistment you must take the ASVAB (Armed Services Vocational Aptitude Battery), an aptitude test that provides you with information about where your strengths lie. The aptitude tests help the Army decide where you are likeliest to fit within the service, and it also can help you narrow your own career choices.

Promotion Requirements
- To private (E-2)—six months active duty and commander recommendation. (In exceptional cases, the commander may accelerate promotions to E-2, E-3, and E-4. For military pay chart information, see Chapter 7.)
- To private first class (E-3)—twelve months active duty service, four months as a private and commander's recommendation.
- To specialist or corporal (E-4)—twelve months active duty service, six months in grade and commander's recommendation.

- To sergeant and staff sergeant (E-5 and E-6)—test against peers in job skill and other soldier skills. Must also have high school diploma and meet Army promotion point system scores and promotion board criteria.
- To sergeant first class and above (E-7 to E-9)—must meet Army centralized selection board criteria.

Officer Programs

If you plan to go through college or participate in one of the many Army officer-training programs, you can carve out a worthwhile career and enjoy the advantages of attaining officer status.

Responsibilities of Being an Officer

What is involved in being an officer? Much responsibility. Depending on an officer's rank, the Army places its commissioned personnel in charge of both soldiers and machines. For the individual officer, this could mean being responsible for only a handful of soldiers or, perhaps, for hundreds of thousands of soldiers. In time of war, officers must make decisions that ultimately will impact others' lives. Along with the responsibility, though, being an officer has advantages.

To begin with, officers earn more money than do enlisted personnel. Officers also are provided with comfortable on-post housing for themselves and their families. If housing is not available on post, officers are given an extra living allowance to help pay for off-post housing.

As previously mentioned, in addition to the programs that train officers, direct appointments are available for men and women who are professionally qualified in certain fields. One of the most popular officer programs for which training is required is that associated with aviation.

Army Aviation Opportunities

In 1911 the Army had one plane and one pilot. Today the Army has thousands of helicopters and operates heliports in the United States and abroad. To run this vast fleet of aircraft and supporting airfields, the Army needs aviators, crew members, mechanics, avionics experts, air traffic controllers, radar operators, and technicians. Trained enlisted personnel fill many of the positions. Aviators, however, who receive more than $450,000 worth of flight training over a period of fifty weeks, earn the rank of aviator/ warrant officer. They are then ready to assume flying duties in the United States or overseas.

The Army's flight training program, which is open to men and women, is tough and physically demanding. It can be emotionally draining as well. As a pilot trainee, you learn how to hide a two-and-a-half-ton helicopter in a tree; how to fly through total darkness to sneak up on a target; how to fly through storms; and, most important of all, how to keep cool under intense pressure. Once you have earned your wings, you will have gained the technical knowledge to be a skilled pilot and the confidence and discipline to be a leader. Aviators are obligated to serve for six years following the date of their commissioning.

Chaplains and Medical Specialists

If you aspire to be a military chaplain, you must meet certain requirements. You must have certain undergraduate credits from an accredited college or university, possess a master of divinity degree (or equivalent theological degree), or have completed sufficient graduate-level study in theology or related subjects to qualify you to perform professional functions as a chaplain. Contact a recruiter to obtain further information and discuss your own situation.

You may obtain a direct appointment in one of the Army's medical administration and field medical operations specialties if you have a baccalaureate degree in a management or health care related area. As an allied health scientist, you may receive a direct appointment in one of the Army's many health career fields if you possess a qualifying graduate degree. Special areas of interest include clinical psychology, pharmacy, optometry, and sanitary engineering. The Army also needs veterinarians—not to treat animals, but to inspect the huge quantities of meat that is fed to the troops.

Space limitations prevent describing every training course the Army has to offer or every opportunity the service can offer you as an enlisted soldier or officer. For further information about the Army and the opportunities that await you in the regular service force, consult your nearest Army recruiter or write to Headquarters, U.S. Army Recruiting Command, Fort Knox, Kentucky 40121-2726; phone (800) USA-ARMY; or access the Army online at http://www.army.mil.

Army National Guard

The National Guard dates back to the very beginning of our nation. Article I, Section 8 of the Constitution provides that the Congress shall have the power to call forth "the Militia to execute the Laws of the Union, suppress insurrections and repel invasions." Although Congress was authorized to organize, arm, and discipline the militia, training and the appointment of officers were left to the states.

The Second Amendment places the National Guard under state jurisdiction in peacetime and permits its use to put down local disturbances. This was true in the case of the 1967 riots in Detroit, Michigan, and Newark, New Jersey. In wartime, however, the National Guard becomes part of the United States military service, and it was mobilized during the Korean War and again in 1961 during the Berlin Crisis. In the 2004 invasion of Iraq and its aftermath, the National Guard supplied a large number of combatants—particularly military police officers. Membership in the National Guard is voluntary, and the federal government pays members for the time spent in drilling and training in the field.

Job opportunities in the National Guard include many of the areas found in the regular Army. Enlistment age is seventeen to thirty-four, but those under eighteen must have the consent of their parents. Applicants must have at least a ninth grade education and, in some cases, may attend basic training before they graduate from high school. Initial training covers basic and advanced skill specialties. While a member is on active duty training, she or he receives full pay and other privileges. After that, monthly and annual training is required during the remainder of the enlistment period.

The Army National Guard also has its own officer-training program for those who are qualified. These officers-in-training attend the same schools and receive the same education as officer candidates in the regular Army. Once training is completed, the officers are commissioned as second lieutenants in the Reserve of the United States. Officers can also be appointed to the Army National Guard after finishing college ROTC. Some men and women may receive a direct appointment if they have certain necessary skills or training, and officers leaving active Army duty may also be appointed to the National Guard.

Civilian Employment Opportunities

In addition to the enlisted and officer personnel, thousands of U.S. citizen employees are engaged in different occupations as members of the Army's worldwide civilian workforce. Every year many of these civilian employment vacancies must be filled, varying from the lowest grade level to executives.

Today's Army offers a broad range of civilian employment opportunities for people of diverse backgrounds, educational achievements, work interests, and job skills. The Army is committed to achieving full equality of opportunity through affirmative action programs that include the Federal Women's Program, the Hispanic Employment Program, and the Upward Mobility Program. (For more information see Chapter 9.)

5

THE AIR FORCE

WHEN PEOPLE THINK of the Air Force, they almost always associate the service with pilots: fighter jocks; "truck drivers" who fly the heavy transport aircraft; or the somewhat mysterious pilots who fly the secret spy aircraft. But the Air Force is more than just a home for pilots. The youngest of the military services, the Air Force provides a fast and fluid air and space capability that can deliver both force and machinery anywhere in the world within forty-eight hours. The mission requires pilots, of course; but it also needs office workers, mechanics, food service specialists, photographers, and just about any other type of support worker used by its sister services. All these types of personnel support a service that flies missions into all except five countries the world over.

Air Force missions include fighting wars, but they also include peacekeeping, medical, and humanitarian assignments. After the devastating earthquake-induced tsunami of December 2004, for instance, the Air Force was fast on the ground to Sri Lanka to assess what was needed in terms of disaster relief. Air Force personnel dispatched emergency meals to victims in Southeast Asia and utilized its C-130 Hercules cargo craft to ferry in emergency supplies. Air Force personnel also participate in search and rescue missions, special operations, and ceremonial duties. If you are interested in learning more about this air-centered service that does much work on the ground, read ahead.

A Comparatively Young Service

Until World War I broke out in 1914, the speed of warfare was determined by how fast foot soldiers could travel and battleships could plow through the seas. Armies and navies were the chief instruments of war until the first primitive, flimsy airplanes appeared over the battlefields of France and changed the future of warfare—and the world. Thirty years later, by the end of World War II, military strategists knew that a nation must be in control of the skies before either the ground forces or the navy could operate safely.

Responsibility for ensuring the safety of the soldiers and sailors belongs to the United States Air Force. Its origins go back to 1907, when the Army Signal Corps established an aeronautical division and purchased its first plane from the Wright Brothers. This craft cost $30,000 (a warplane now costs more than a million dollars) and was capable of flying at a speed of forty-two and a half miles an hour (today's fighters fly at Mach 2). Only ten years later, daring American and German World War I aviators engaged in dogfights. Even so, air power did not decide the outcome of the war.

Nevertheless, after the armistice, Billy Mitchell, an army brigadier general who had organized and commanded the American air force, arranged for a sensational bombing and sinking of several obsolete warships to show the importance of the Army's air force. Because Mitchell criticized military leaders for neglecting air power, he was court-martialed. In 1926 he was sentenced to a five-year suspension from duty without pay. He resigned and continued his campaign for air power. His ideas were not adopted until Hitler's Luftwaffe dominated the skies at the outbreak of World War II in 1939. With America's entry into the conflict, the Army air forces assumed a major role in the Allies' military plans to win the war against Germany, Italy, and Japan.

The Glamour Service

The U.S. Air Force has the reputation for being the "glamour service." The nation's youngest military branch, the Air Force began as part of the Army. It originally was called the Army Air Corps and saw extensive service in World War II. After the war ended, the Air Force became its own distinct branch. It came into being on September 18, 1947. At that point, the newly formed service took ownership of all the aircraft, facilities, personnel, and property it had used while still part of the Army. The brand new Department of the Air Force became responsible for defending the nation against air attack. Now it continues to conduct air warfare, providing both combat and logistical support to the Army. It also cooperates with the other services in joint operations. However, this is only part of the story.

The United States Air Force performs myriad duties, only some of which are covered here. For example, the Air Force serves as the first line of defense against missiles directed at North America and is constantly guarding against a surprise air or missile attack. It operates early warning systems, such as Space Command's NORAD, the North American Air Defense system based at Cheyenne Mountain near Colorado Springs, Colorado. NORAD provides air defense both for the United States and Canada. Elsewhere, crews at Arctic outposts, on shipboard, and in long-range search planes constantly watch for signs of enemy attack, while interceptor aircraft are ever on the alert to destroy bombers that might arrive following an air attack.

The Air Force Special Operations Command has a force that integrates ground combat with air operations. Troops assigned to this command participate in personnel recovery missions, such as rescuing pilots trapped behind enemy lines; or work alongside other services' special operations forces, such as Navy SEALs or Army Rangers. This command also employs combat weathermen—a unique type of weather forecaster who gathers and analyzes weather data that would have an impact on combat forces. The Air Force handles this task on behalf of U.S. Army soldiers.

The Air Force has had an ongoing role in operations in Afghanistan. The mission started on a small scale, with gravel roads surrounding temporary wooden huts that housed a relative handful of people. Now the unit in question—the 455th Air Expeditionary Wing—has more permanent buildings and concrete roads and is likely to remain in place for years, providing aerial cover for ground troops in Afghanistan.

In other positions around the globe, members of the Air Force must remain alert every single minute, both day and night, in good weather and in bad, protecting our nation from unexpected attack. Members of the service might find themselves flying over the North Pole in a weather observation plane, piloting a jet fighter that is based somewhere in Europe, or working in a missile test center in California.

In addition to these traditional types of duties, the Air Force also has handled a far more unusual assignment: tracking UFOs, otherwise known as Unidentified Flying Objects. In an extensive study lasting from 1947 through 1969, the Air Force investigated some

12,618 UFO sightings. Although the service no longer operates "Project Blue Book," it happily provides information to people still curious about the 701 remaining unsolved sightings.

Air Force Commands

As with all the other services, the Air Force is organized into multiple commands, each governing a type of duty or a field of responsibility. Space Command—as its name implies—handles matters pertaining to aerospace. Air Education and Training Command governs the various schools. Air Force Materiel Command provides equipment and goods.

Since flying airplanes is the most important activity of the Air Force, it would seem natural to start a career review with a look at flying officers.

Air Force Flying Officers

Flying officers are generally of two types: pilots and navigators.

Pilots

Air Force pilots are among aviation's elite. Intelligent and in excellent physical condition, they are responsible and mature. They operate multimillion-dollar defense aircraft and fly at technology's leading edge. A majority of Air Force commanders wear the silver wings of an Air Force aviator, and many commercial pilots owe their expertise to their Air Force flight training and experience.

Prospective Air Force pilots first go through a fifty-hour introductory course taught by civilian flight instructors. Here the pilot hopefuls learn to fly a small training craft, such as the Cessna 152. In the next phase, Air Force pilots join with their Navy counterparts at a school called Joint Specialized Undergraduate Pilot Training. In this course, conducted at one of several sites, students take on a heavy course load of academic subjects, as well as officer development and physical training classes. They also spend much time in aircraft simulators and in the air.

As the course progresses, each pilot moves into one of a number of tracks to concentrate on flying tanker aircraft, turboprops, helicopters, or fighter-bomber planes. The joint school lasts about fifty-two weeks. The Air Force and Navy pilots then return to their home services and go through additional training in their assigned aircraft. Afterwards they are assigned to an operational unit. A normal assignment may continue for three to four years, at the conclusion of which the pilot may be considered for transfer to a different type of aircraft on a new base.

To qualify for Air Force pilot training, you must be a college graduate. You must not be younger than twenty and one-half years of age or older than twenty-six and one-half at the time of your application. You must be no older than twenty-seven when you enter pilot training. You must be physically and mentally qualified, of good moral character, and a United States citizen.

Navigators

To the educated eyes of the navigator, the radarscope's blur of light, lines, and shadow becomes a clear indication of coastline, land contour, and position.

Aircraft location is the primary concern of the navigator. The wind, weather, speed, heading, and the altitude must be considered. There is no margin for error. The trained navigator can guide the aircraft safely and surely between points hundreds or thousands of miles apart. He or she must be able to produce detailed flight plans for thousands of nautical miles in only minutes. A flight plan must be completed to tolerances of one pound of fuel, one foot of altitude, one-tenth of a minute in time, and one-tenth of a minute in latitude and longitude—a tall order.

As a navigator trainee, you begin with the basic foundation of air navigation—dead reckoning. You learn to maintain an accurate record of time, speed, direction, and wind effect, using them to determine the exact position of the aircraft without references to landmarks. You study map reading, radar, day and night celestial, inertial, radio, and low-level navigation. There are courses in weather, aviation physiology, flight instruments, aircraft flight regulations, and integrated navigation systems.

To be considered for navigator training, you must be a college graduate. You must be not younger than eighteen years of age or older than twenty-seven when you enter navigation training. You must be physically and mentally qualified, of good moral character, and a United States citizen.

Other Career Areas on a Professional Level

Technology touches virtually every aspect of the Air Force mission. Jobs are available in many scientific, engineering, or technology-oriented fields. These include mechanical engineering, communications, electronics, computer systems, and civil engineering.

Because the Air Force spends billions of dollars a year on civilian contracts for new electronic systems, aircraft, and space vehicles, it depends on its officer scientists and engineers for the overall leadership, management, and coordination of these projects. As a service member holding this type of job, you will have an excellent opportunity to start out in a management position, making tough technical decisions and developing important professional associations. You will acquire priceless experience and assume increasing responsibility. At the same time, you may have a chance to work on supersophisticated projects and lay a solid foundation for a successful and rewarding career.

The Air Force has a comprehensive health care program, so dentists, physicians, and nurses are in great demand. It offers many unusual personal and professional opportunities for those with medical training. Many other professional skills are needed. If you are contemplating professional training or have a professional degree, discuss it with an Air Force recruiter. Find out how you might carve out a career.

There are three ways you can become an Air Force science and engineering officer: ROTC (see Chapter 8), the Air Force Academy (see Chapter 8), and officer training school. The latter offers an intensive twelve-week course for the college graduate. General eligibility requirements are that you must be between the ages of eighteen and thirty (which can be waived up to age thirty-five), in good physical condition, and of good moral character. You must meet Air Force officer qualifying criteria and hold a degree from an accredited college or university. Applicants must be U.S. citizens.

Opportunities for Enlisted Air Personnel

Young people who enter the Air Force find that—as with the other services—training begins on the premise that they have a solid high school background. Also like the other services, the Air Force requires all potential enlistees to take a universal first step: the aptitude and qualification exams. Although this may sound daunting to some, the tests are not overly difficult. Anyone who has attained a high school diploma will have the skills needed to complete the military entrance exam. The main value of these tests is to help both you and service personnel accurately assess your particular strengths and abilities and to determine where you will best fit within the military.

The Air Force test contains questions designed to help find people with the technical skills required to work on aviation-related computers and machinery.

Your own examination results will be entered into a computer. The computer program will analyze your abilities and aptitudes and will produce a list of skills for which there are openings. From this list, you will choose the skill you want before you enter training. If you have trouble narrowing your choices, your recruiter is trained to help you find the information that will help you make the best decision.

Once you choose a career field, your recruiter will tell you when your particular school has an opening and when you will need to report for in-processing to the Air Force.

If there are no immediate openings, you may enter the delayed enlistment program. This program permits you to enlist and wait up to twelve months for an opening. Some enlistees will enter this program in order to attend their desired school—or, if they are flexible about their choice of school but are eager to join the service right away, they will switch to another school that has immediate openings. Just keep in mind that if you cannot get the school you want when you want it, the Air Force can offer alternatives. Be sure to discuss this with your recruiter to learn all the options.

Minimum age for enlisting is eighteen (seventeen with parental consent) and the maximum age is twenty-seven. High school graduates are preferred, but lack of a high school diploma will not disbar you necessarily from qualifying for the Air Force. Discuss your educational background with the recruiter.

Once you sign up to join the Air Force, your first stop—no matter what service school you plan to attend—is basic training.

Basic Training

Basic training, which takes six weeks, is explained in the Air Force booklet titled, simply enough, *Basic Training*. The following excerpt gives a good overview of the program.

> Divided into four parts: in-processing, military training, academic training, and evaluation (yours and theirs). They all blend into one another from one week to the next. Physical conditioning begins slowly, but you'll be jogging a mile in eight minutes before you leave. And you'll do some other simple exercises and drill, and you'll trim down and harden up and feel better. Proud. Two hours of PT a day does that for you.
>
> And you'll familiarize yourself with a rifle, run a confidence course, and take a test over the things you've learned in the class-room; things like Air Force history, customs, courtesies, first aid, and human relations. You won't have any trouble with it.
>
> Your last week will slip up on you. And you'll be asked to eval-uate your training and, if you have some good suggestions, changes will result. Honest. Then you'll hit the parade field one more time for a final review. It's over. You've made it. You shake hands with your squadron commander and your TI. Your orders for school or that first duty assignment are waiting for you. You know where you're going by now. . . . You're part of a modern ser-vice geared for a modern man. You know what you're doing and a whole lot more about yourself. That's what basic is all about.

The next step, as with all services, is specialized training. The length of these courses varies according to the type of job you will have in the Air Force. The courses can be both demanding and invaluable.

Specialized Training

In just eleven weeks' time, for example, an airman can become a jet engine mechanic who is capable of walking into a jet engine repair shop ready to work. This knowledge will stay with the airman whether he or she remains with the Air Force or eventually seeks a job at an airline or manufacturer.

With proper guidance and encouragement from the instructor, Air Force students literally teach themselves. They must, however, understand and be able to apply the principles they learn. Many of the courses are self-paced, which allows the students to progress at their own speed through a specific course of required skills.

Promotion Requirements

Note: Recruiters also have information on STEP and Below-the-Zone promotions. For more information about the military pay chart, see Chapter 7.

- To airman (E-2)—airman basic must have six months in grade and commander recommendation.
- To airman first class (E-3)—airman must have ten months in grade and commander recommendation.
- To senior airman (E-4)—airman must have thirty-six months in service and twenty months in grade or twenty-eight months in grade.
- To staff sergeant (E-5), technical sergeant (E-6), and master sergeant (E-7)—based on time in grade/time in-service requirements and points. Performance reports, decorations, job knowledge, and Air Force knowledge tests also earn points toward promotion. Compete against others in same grade and job skill.
- To senior and chief master sergeant (E-8 and E-9)—virtually the same as E-5 and above. Also must meet a selection board based on whole-person concept.

Occupational Fields

Here's a look at just some of the occupational fields in which enlisted personnel are trained and employed. As you will see, some are specific to the airborne mission; others are not.

Accounting, finance, and auditing
Administrative
Aircrew protection
Audiovisual
Band
Computer systems operations
Counterintelligence
Dental
Intelligence
Mechanical/electrical
Missile electronics maintenance
Morale, welfare, and recreation
Motor vehicle maintenance
Munitions and weapons maintenance
Personnel
Photomapping
Public affairs
Sanitation
Security police
Special investigations
Supply services
Transportation
Weather

Let's take just two of these fields to see what is involved and how the skills can be used both in and out of the military.

Audiovisual
- **Duties and responsibilities.** Operates aerial and ground camera, motion picture, and other photographic equipment; processes photographs and film; edits motion pictures; performs photographic instrumentation functions; and operates airborne, field, and precision processing laboratories.
- **Qualifications.** Considerable dexterity on small precision equipment, excellent eyesight. Mathematics, physics, and chemistry desirable.
- **Examples of civilian jobs.** Camera operator, darkroom technician, film editor, aerial commercial photographer, photograph finisher, sound mixer, and motion picture operator.

Computer Systems Operations
- **Duties and responsibilities.** Collects, processes, records, prepares, and submits data for various automated systems; analyzes, designs, programs, and operates computer systems.
- **Qualifications.** Business arithmetic, algebra, and geometry desirable.
- **Examples of civilian jobs.** Card-type converter or computer operator, data typist, data processing control clerk, high-speed printer operator, programmer.

For additional occupational information, see Appendix D.

For More Information

Contact the nearest Air Force recruiting officer. This information is listed in your telephone directory under the heading United States Government. Or, write to Headquarters, USAF Recruiting Service (RSOO), Randolph Air Force Base, Texas 78150, or call (800) 423-USAF. For a comprehensive look at what the Air Force has to offer, check out its informative website and helpful links at http://www.af.mil.

6

THE COAST GUARD

THE UNITED STATES Coast Guard is the oldest continuous maritime government agency. It's slogan—*semper paratus*—means "always prepared."

After the Revolutionary War, the Continental Navy was disbanded. From 1790 until 1798, when the United States Navy was established, the Treasury Department's Revenue Marine Division cutters were the nation's only maritime force. Alexander Hamilton, Secretary of the Treasury, had persuaded the new Congress to create a Revenue Marine, to combat piracy and stop smuggling into the original thirteen states. It was urgent that the tariff laws be enforced. Duties on imports were then the principal revenue for the new country. The law that later established the Navy also empowered the president to use the revenue cutters to supplement the naval fleet when needed in time of war. In 1863 the name of the organization was changed to Revenue Cutter Service and in 1915 to Coast Guard.

Since 1790 the Coast Guard has grown from the first tiny fleet of ten revenue cutters to a large force of helicopters, airplanes, and ships. Its members have fought in most of the wars and have rescued thousands of women, men, and children. They have saved billions of dollars worth of property from destruction by floods and shipwrecks. They began as a few hardy sailors who manned those first ten ships cruising along the Atlantic coastal waters. Now the service has expanded its activities within the United States and around most of the world.

Its work is often dangerous and the risks are great. The women and men who join the Coast Guard make a serious commitment. This is evident by the motto: "You have to go out, but you don't have to come back."

The mission of the Coast Guard Recruit Training Center is to train young men and women to be always prepared to serve in the sky and at sea, with courage, alertness, and devotion, eager to learn the skills and traditions of the United States Coast Guard in the service of their country and humanity.

Coast Guard Activities

As the principal organization for protecting life and property at sea as well as enforcing our maritime laws, the Coast Guard has a broad range of interesting responsibilities. A typical day can find the Coast Guard involved in a variety of situations. For example, on one day in May a Canadian tightrope walker attempted to walk a 2,670-foot cable some 200 feet above the Mississippi River near New Orleans. High winds caused him to lose control. His seventy-pound balancing pole fell to the water and he clung to the cable until a Coast Guard boat came to his rescue.

Meanwhile, farther up the river a captain was steering his cutter along a three-hundred-mile stretch between St. Louis, Missouri, and Davenport, Iowa. Four other Coast Guard vessels were sailing elsewhere on the river. They dropped anchor from time to time so the crews could change light bulbs in light towers, inspect bridges, retrieve missing buoys torn from their moorings, and clear brush from around navigation lights on the shore. The crews' workday started at six in the morning and ended at dark. A midnight oil spill or a predawn rescue would keep them from their bunks.

Up at the Coast Guard Academy in New London, Connecticut, 164 newly commissioned officers who had just finished their four-year college training were tossing their hats up in the air. This concluded their graduation ceremony, which featured an address by then Vice President Bush. One of the graduates, Helen Louise Holtzman, had special reason for being proud. When she arrived at the ceremony, three members of her family were watching: her grandfather, George W. Holtzman, a retired Coast Guard captain, class of 1933; her father, Captain Edward B. Holtzman, class of 1957; and her sister, Lieutenant Virginia K. Holtzman, class of 1981. The ceremony was special for another reason: Angela Dennis and Daphne Reese became the first black women to graduate from the Academy, just three years after the first white woman received her commission.

As the new officers were flinging their hats up above them, a cutter was patrolling in the general region of the Newfoundland Grand Banks. It was looking for icebergs and ice fields. Ice observation starts in February and ends in July. From April until July the area, about the size of Pennsylvania, is blanketed by dangerous fog. It is created by the confluence of the Gulf Stream and the Labrador Current. However, not a single ship has been lost to ice in this patrolled area since fifteen hundred people perished when the *Titanic* was struck and sunk by an iceberg in 1912. Icebreaking is another responsibility of the Coast Guard. Its ships work the Arctic as well as the Great Lakes and adjacent rivers.

Far to the south outside Miami, another cutter hove to a ship that it had stopped. The captain suspected that this was another attempt to smuggle drugs into the country from South America. Back in New London, Vice President Bush was commenting on this very activity of the service, which he felt showed great "professionalism and courage." He told the graduates: "Drug smuggling is a multibillion dollar business. Some of these smugglers equip what amounts to private armies to protect their investments." Smugglers often decide to fight it out rather than surrender, he added, and many of these ships have more guns than Coast Guard cutters carry.

Elsewhere the Alaskan patrol was on duty, helping protect the fisheries by enforcing provisions of the two-hundred-mile offshore fish conservation act. In several large harbors other members of the service were working to keep the waterfront safe by controlling pollution, dangerous cargoes, and traffic.

In various ports safety officers were boarding and inspecting United States flag merchant vessels and some foreign vessels. They checked cargo stowage, the seaworthiness of the ships, their pollution abatement, material safety, and whether safety standards were being observed. Other personnel were investigating violations, marine accidents, and cases of misconduct or negligence on the part of sailors or ships' officers. Some were testing, licensing, and certifying merchant marine personnel and other vessel-operating personnel. All these activities were going on in one day.

The search and rescue responsibility of the Coast Guard dates back to 1831, when the secretary of the treasury directed the revenue cutter *Gallatin* to cruise the coast in search of persons in distress. This was the first time a government agency was specifically charged with searching for those who might be in danger. The records of the lifesaving crews are crowded with remarkable rescues. The following are examples.

- The schooners *Robert Wallace* and *David Wallace* were wrecked at Marquette, Michigan, on November 18, 1886. The Ship Canal Station crew traveled 110 miles by special train and rescued the ships' crews.
- In three days' work on the Delaware coast, September 10–12, 1889, the lifesaving crews at Lewes, Henlopen, and Rehoboth Beach stations assisted twenty-two vessels and rescued 39 persons by boat and 155 by breeches buoy without losing a single life.
- The British schooner *H.P. Kirkham* was wrecked on Rose and Crown Shoal on January 2, 1892. The crew of seven was rescued after fifteen hours of exposure, but the lifesaving crew was at sea in an open boat without food for twenty-three hours.
- More recently, in October 1980, the Dutch cruise ship *Prinsendam* was jarred by explosions after a fire started in the engine room. In spite of rough seas and strong winds, four Coast Guard, one Air Force, and two Canadian helicopters plucked more than five hundred shipwrecked survivors from crowded lifeboats in the cold Alaskan Gulf. Many of the survivors, mostly senior citizens, were lifted in rescue blankets to the awaiting Coast Guard cutter *Boutwell* and a nearby commercial tanker. Not one life was lost; the *Prinsendam* sank seven days later.

The surfboat was the primary rescue vehicle from 1848 until the development of the helicopter following World War II. Today it is possible to save many more lives. This is thanks to the ability of the helicopter to reach vessels in distress quickly and perform rescue work. Thus this aircraft has emerged as a primary rescue tool.

Opportunities for Enlistees

You can sign up for the Coast Guard now and wait up to six months to join. You may wait for a year if you are in school. The advantage of doing this is that the time between the day you sign up and the day you report for duty counts toward your seniority for pay.

Recruit Training

An unusual feature of this service is its buddy plan. This is for you and a friend (of the same sex). It guarantees that you can go through boot camp (basic training) together. This entails eight tough weeks at Cape May, New Jersey, or Alameda, California (women attend only Cape May). It consists of rigorous physical training and practical classroom work. It also includes orientation about Coast Guard history, its mission, and the basics of seamanship. Boot camp exposes you to discipline to help you better handle responsibility. It teaches what you have to do and then makes sure you're able to do it efficiently as part of a team. Lives and property are going to depend on how well you learn the necessary and basic skills during these two months.

Boot camp is not all classes and calisthenics. There is still enough free time to make new friends, write letters, enjoy three meals a day, and get plenty of sleep. There are recreational facilities, gymnasiums for basketball and volleyball, and, naturally, swimming pools.

Once those eight weeks are over, you can expect about ten days of leave so you can go home.

Seaman recruits receive pay according to the E-1 classification; those recruits with dependents receive an additional allowance for housing and may send money home at regular intervals. After graduation, pay jumps to the next level in the pay scale.

Once boot camp is over and you report back for duty, you have two choices. You can request either an on-the-job assignment or admission to Coast Guard school for specialized training.

If you choose the work route, you could find yourself stationed in New Orleans, New York, Seattle, or one of many other locations. You might be providing navigational aids to ore carriers, grain barges, or oceangoing container ships. You might be enforcing boating safety regulations off the Florida coast. Then you could be part of a search and rescue team on the Pacific coast. There you would soon be answering calls for help from capsized sailboats or stricken large merchant ships. You might be a crewman on an icebreaker in the Great Lakes or you may be enforcing the two-hundred-mile offshore fish conservation act. You might even end up fighting pollution and protecting the environment from chemical, oil, or sewage spills. You may designate your choice while in boot camp. The Coast Guard will do its best to honor your wishes, but it cannot guarantee to do so.

One advantage of choosing a work-and-learn program is that it gives you a chance to obtain a more general knowledge of what the Coast Guard does. Then you can decide which would be the right course of study for you. Alternatively, you can work toward achieving a petty officer status by performing your on-the-job duties, completing correspondence courses in your chosen specialty, and passing a written examination. Once you achieve petty officer status, advancement is based on a servicewide system of competition where each officer competes with her or his peers for available positions. Promotions depend on your initiative and skill, so it is really up to you.

Promotion Requirements

- To seaman recruit (E-2)—upon completion of basic training.
- To seaman or firearm (E-3)—based on adequate time in grade (six months), demonstration of military and professional qualifications, recommendation by commanding officer, and completion of correspondence courses.
- To petty officer ratings (E-4 through E-9)—must pass the Coast Guard–wide competitive examination for the rating, complete service schooling, or progress through on-the-job training. For military pay chart information, see Chapter 7.

Technical Training

Suppose you have chosen to attend school after boot camp. There are many specialist ratings or classifications open to you in four groupings:

- **Deck and ordnance group.** Boatswain's mate, quartermaster, radar man, sonar technician, gunner's mate, fire control technician.
- **Hull and engineering group.** Damage control man, machinery technician, electronics technician, telephone technician, electrician's mate.
- **Aviation group.** Aviation machinist mate, aviation survival man, aviation electronics technician, aviation electrician's mate, aviation structural mechanic.

- **Administration and scientific group.** Marine science technician, yeoman, storekeeper, radioman, subsistence specialist, port security man, health services technician, public affairs specialist.

Following below are more detailed descriptions of a few of these ratings.

Boatswain's Mate

This is the master seaman, a person skilled in all phases of seamanship and in handling deck force personnel. This person frequently acts as officer in charge of patrol boats, tugs, small craft, port security teams, and small shore units. The boatswain's mate is also capable of performing almost any task in connection with the operation of small boats, navigation, entering or leaving port, storing cargo, and handling ropes and lines.

Boatswain's mates must be leaders, be physically strong, and have good hearing and vision. They should possess a high degree of manual dexterity. Courses in algebra, geometry, and shop are helpful. Previous experience handling small boats is extremely valuable. Training is achieved either through ten weeks of intensive study at the Coast Guard Reserve Training Center in Yorktown, Virginia, or by training on the job under the guidance of experienced personnel and studying appropriate manuals and publications.

Related civilian jobs include pier superintendent, tugboat crewman, heavy equipment operator, ship pilot, and marina supervisor.

Radar Man

No one knows how many ships have avoided collisions or bad weather or how many distressed vessels have been located because of a highly skilled radar man. This person operates all types of radar equipment to search for, locate, and track the movement of ships, aircraft, and other surface objects.

Radar men should be able to use numbers in practical problems and have good vision, normal hearing, and a clear voice. A good background in mathematics and shop courses in both radio and electricity are helpful, as is experience in operating ham radio systems. Training begins either with seventeen weeks at Navy Operations Specialist School at Dam Neck, Virginia, or on the job being guided by experienced personnel while studying appropriate manuals and publications. Related civilian jobs include radio operator, control room manager, air traffic controller, and missile tracking specialist.

Damage Control Man

This specialist is responsible for preserving the safety and survival devices on all Coast Guard vessels. Duties include, among other things, welding, firefighting, pipefitting, and woodworking. Training begins either with thirteen weeks of specialized study at the Coast Guard Reserve Training Center in Yorktown, Virginia, or by performing on-the-job training and studying training course manuals and other publications.

Related civilian jobs include firefighter, carpenter, construction foreman, safety engineer, building superintendent, and machinist.

Aviation Electronics Technician

This man or woman is responsible for the operational condition of all radio, radar, and other electronic devices that are used for rapid communications, controlled landing approaches, detection of distressed vessels, and efficient navigation. You should be proficient in solving practical mathematical problems and have a high degree of electrical and mechanical aptitude. School courses in algebra, trigonometry, physics, electricity, and mechanics are useful. Also helpful is practical experience in the electrical trades. Training begins with twenty-four weeks of intensive training at the Coast Guard Aviation Technical Training Center in Elizabeth City, North Carolina.

Related civilian jobs include aircraft electrician, aircraft communications specialist, radio and radar repairer, computer technician, and radio operator.

Yeoman

Efficient administration depends on the efficient performance of a highly trained clerical staff. The yeoman fills that need as he or she prepares, records, and keeps the Coast Guard's vast number of letters, messages, and reports flowing smoothly. Yeomen also operate a variety of automated data and word processing equipment. Qualifications for this position are similar to those of secretaries, stenographers, and typists in private industry. Yeomen should possess a degree of manual dexterity and be able to work harmoniously with others in an office. Courses in English and in business subjects such as typing and filing are very useful. Some knowledge of word processing and similar programs would be helpful. Training begins either with ten weeks instruction at the Coast Guard Training Center in Petaluma, California, or by performing on-the-job duties under the direction of an experienced yeoman while studying specially designed manuals.

Related civilian jobs include executive secretary, personnel manager, court reporter, and legal clerk.

Health Services Technician

This individual carries responsibility for the health of her or his shipmates. The health services technician also plays an important role in lifesaving. He or she learns human anatomy and physiology, chemistry, pharmacy, dentistry, preventive medicine, and medical administration. A corpsman should have a pleasing personality and a desire to help those in need of medical attention as well as be able to solve practical mathematical problems. School courses in hygiene, biology, physiology, chemistry, typing, and public speaking are definite assets. Experience in first aid groups is valuable. Training starts with twenty-four weeks of instruction and practical application at the Coast Guard Academy in New London, Connecticut.

Some related civilian jobs include X-ray technician, medical technician, pharmaceutical salesperson, and physician's or dentist's assistant.

Port Security Man

This specialist supervises and controls the safe handling, transportation, and storage of explosives and other dangerous cargoes. He or she is well versed in the regulations and equipment and is responsible for the safety of vessels, harbors, and other waterfront facilities. This person is expert in the field of preventing and extinguishing fire. A port security man should be average or above in general learning ability and have normal hearing and vision. School courses in practical mathematics, chemistry, and English are helpful. Any prior experience in law enforcement is extremely beneficial. Ten weeks of intensive training begins at the Coast Guard Reserve Training Center in Yorktown, Virginia.

Related civilian jobs include insurance investigator, firefighter, pier superintendent, and warehouseman.

The port security man rating is open only to members of the Coast Guard Reserve. The recruiting officer can give you the latest information about joining the Reserve.

If you want to enlist in the Coast Guard, you must be a United States citizen and be between the ages of seventeen and twenty-six. You must meet certain physical, mental, and character standards, and a high school diploma is highly recommended.

Officer Candidates

Here is what the Coast Guard says about officer candidates:

> Because the missions of the Coast Guard are so important and demanding, the service wants top-notch officers who won't wilt under pressure.
>
> Many of these officers are obtained through officer candidate school. They are graduates of a highly specialized, seventeen-week course in leadership, seamanship, navigation, law enforcement, and military subjects. Classes convene about four times a year at the Coast Guard Reserve Training Center in Yorktown, Virginia. Graduates are commissioned as ensigns and serve on active duty for three years. Those who wish may apply for integration into the regular Coast Guard and, if accepted, continue to serve in a proud and challenging service.
>
> While attending officer candidate school you may indicate the type of duty and location you prefer after graduation. Your wishes will be taken into consideration along with the needs of the service, your experience, and your educational background.
>
> Not all of the jobs are ashore. Junior officers serve as underway watch officers on ships ranging in size from 100 feet long to the 378-foot gas turbine-powered, high-endurance cutters. It is

here your training in seamanship, ship handling, navigation, and leadership will be needed the most.

Coast Guard ships operate from the tropics to the ice masses at both poles. Besides the satisfaction of serving at sea, there is the excitement of visiting new ports and making new friends.

Some of the duties graduates of officer candidate school might be assigned include: industrial management, port safety/law enforcement, Reserve administration, naval engineering, civil engineering, financial and supply management, military readiness, data processing, research and development, public affairs, search and rescue, aviation, environmental protection, personnel administration, communications management, boating safety, Coast Guard auxiliary liaison, intelligence, Merchant Marine safety, recruit training, personnel recruitment, civil rights.

Duty stations run the gamut from a small station in Alaska or Hawaii to port safety units in major ports. Many OCS graduates are assigned to bases, district offices, and at headquarters, where their prior experience and specialized educational background are immediately put to use.

Competition for the officer candidate school is stiff. You must be at least twenty-one years of age and under twenty-seven by a cutoff date established twice a year. You must be a citizen of the United States, be of good moral character, and meet physical standards prescribed for original entry into the service. You must have a baccalaureate degree from an accredited college or university. The United States Public Health Service provides dentists and physicians serving in the Coast Guard, and the United States Navy assigns chaplains. The Coast Guard also commissions a limited number of prior service aviators who are graduates of a United States military flight-training program and have had civilian or military flying experience.

A Heroic Rescue

One final gripping illustration of how the Coast Guard serves took place out on the West Coast one stormy afternoon. The radio operator at the Yaquina Bay Coast Guard Station in Newport, Oregon, tensed as he listened to the skipper calling from a small pleasure craft.

"Just spotted an overturned trawler, seas running high, about twelve miles southwest of Newport."

"Were there any survivors?" the operator asked as he wrote 6:30 P.M. in his log.

"No, couldn't see them if they were there. Storm's getting worse."

Minutes later Coast Guard Rescue Helicopter 1353 was in the air heading for the vessel. Lieutenant Al Seidel, the pilot, soon spotted the keel of the *Odyssey* rocking violently in ten-foot seas. His companion, Commander Glenn Gunn, reported their discovery and position to the station. In no time, two Coast Guard motor lifeboats started chugging toward them. By the time they arrived an hour later, it was dark and the storm had worsened. Commander Gunn radioed down to the lifeboats and told them there were no survivors but to put a man on the hull just to make certain.

"Nobody could live through this storm, even if they got out of there alive," one of the crewmen observed as the helicopter continued to hover over the motorboats. Suddenly, a hoisting line with a harness dropped to the deck and Petty Officer Craig White seized it. He got into the harness and was swung over to the hull. He dropped and hit it with full force, then grabbed onto the keel. Using a small hammer he pounded on the steel, put his ear to the metal, and listened. Above the roar of the wind and waves, he heard distinct tapping in response. He waved his other arm to signal his discovery. Back at the Newport Station, the Coast Guard again went into action.

Since there were no professional divers among the Coast Guard personnel, officials contacted two local divers, who then volunteered for the rescue mission. As they were flying toward the vessel, the operations officer decided to take no chances. He called the co-owner of a commercial diving company.

"Two divers are on their way now," he explained. Then he asked if the partners would be available to help, if necessary. "We'd like you and your partner to stand by in case we need help."

Two hours later Helicopter 1353 radioed that the divers did not dare to go down into the vessel.

"Let's go," Bill Shires told his partner Pat Miller when he heard the report. They ran toward the waiting helicopter. At 12:30 A.M. they were hovering over the *Odyssey,* peering down through blinding sheets of rain with forty-five-mile-an-hour winds churning the sea and buffeting the aircraft.

"O.K. Let us down," Shires called above the howling wind. The two divers dropped down. Once they were on the keel, they slipped over the side and into the overturned ship. Eventually they found where the two men were trapped. Finally, they led them under water up to the surface—and safety. In recognition of their feat, they were presented the Coast Guard's highest civilian award for valor. For the Coast Guard officers and crewmen, however, it was just another job in the line of duty.

The Coast Guard Reserve

The Coast Guard Reserve offers training in a variety of skills and specialties (called ratings) and is open to anyone age seventeen through thirty-five who can meet the enlistment requirements. Those with prior military service are eligible up to age forty-two.

When you join the Reserve you serve one weekend each month, usually Saturday and Sunday, and two weeks of active duty training every year. You can join the Reserve without prior service, you can join while in high school or college and train during summers, or—if you are out of school and have been working at a trade for a few years, are age twenty-six through thirty-five, and have a skill the Coast Guard can use—you can enter directly as a petty officer with the responsibility and pay that goes with it.

As a member of the Reserve you get a monthly paycheck, can earn retirement benefits and money toward an education, attend Coast Guard technical schools to learn new skills or polish old ones, and enjoy some privileges at military commissaries and exchanges. Best of all, you can continue your civilian life and regular career and serve only one weekend a month plus two weeks a year, unless called up for other duty. You must serve a minimum of eight years after joining, but depending upon the program you are in, it might be less.

The Coast Guard During Wartime

The Coast Guard traditionally has performed two roles in wartime. The first has been to augment the Navy with personnel and cutters. The second has been to undertake special missions for which peacetime experiences have prepared the service with unique skills. For example, during World War II, the Coast Guard manned landing craft in every major amphibious operation. Service craft rescued thousands of survivors of torpedo attacks and other marine disasters, patrolled beaches and docks, and sank enemy submarines. More than two thousand died during the conflict. In both the Korean and Vietnam wars, the Coast Guard worked side by side with the other military services, true to its slogan, *semper paratus.*

For more information about the Coast Guard, contact the nearest Coast Guard recruiter. To find out where the office is located, call (800) 424-8883 or go to http://www. gov.info/uscg.

7

Is Military Service for You?

For many of us our work is enjoyable, but we must admit that there are certain aspects that could be improved or removed altogether. Some people are resigned to endure jobs for the simple goal of collecting a paycheck.

The military is not this type of job. For one thing, it provides a vital service: national defense. As such, the military has a strong sense of purpose—a feeling that is imparted even to the newest recruit. Civilian family members are frequently heard to remark that they see a change in their young uniformed family members, even after a short time in service. The fresh recruits seem to have a sense of responsibility and pride in themselves and their country.

The military values its people. It brags about them. The Pentagon routinely calls its service members "our nation's best and brightest." Military leaders strive constantly to instill values: duty, integrity, ethics, honor, courage, and loyalty. These are qualities that society holds in high esteem, and society holds its service members in high esteem.

With those observations in mind, consider some of the advantages and disadvantages of a military career.

Advantages of a Military Career

On the most basic level, from an "employee" point of view, the military offers job security. No matter how sour the economy may be, there always will be a military. There always will be openings for soldiers, sailors, airmen, and Marines. As with other jobs, of course, military personnel must perform well to retain their positions. In times of peace and in poor economy, this can become complicated; some jobs can be eliminated, or people may be weeded out if they fail to rise in rank after a predetermined length of time. But as long as your work and behavior are satisfactory, you will not have to worry about being fired to make room for the nephew of the boss or because someone higher up does not like you. In the military, job retention and loss are handled fairly and equitably.

The military is known as the most egalitarian organization in U.S. society. This means it is fair toward its members, regardless of social class or ethnic background. The military was in the forefront of racial equality, promoting people based not on race but on ability. The military also has been a leader in sexual equality. Even though a number of combat jobs remain closed to females, there are fewer and fewer job fields that do not include women. In fact, more than 95 percent of all military jobs are now open to women. Additionally, women routinely achieve positions based solely on brainpower and leadership ability—particularly in the Army, where women have made tremendous strides in the field of intelligence.

Other advantages cover the basics of day-to-day existence. You will have good living conditions with three adequate meals a day. You will be provided with a wardrobe of military clothing and shoes. If you live on base you will be given a bed, blankets, a pillow, and a place to store your goods. Medical and dental care is available at no cost to you, whether you are working on the post or become ill while home on leave.

High on the list of advantages is the financial aid available for qualified men and women who are eager to obtain further education or a college degree before or during their service. Other educational opportunities await enlistees who wish to study during their spare time. They will find that the government will probably pay 75 to 90 percent of their tuition costs. Another educational plus awaits those who have families and live on military posts. Their children may attend elementary or high schools without payment of school taxes or tuition fees.

Members of the Air Force, for example, may attend the Community College of the Air Force and work toward an associate in applied science degree. The Veterans Educational Assistance Programs allow enlisted members of all services and officers to contribute $25 to $100 a month (up to $2,700), and when the individual is discharged, the government will provide two-for-one matching funds ($5,400 maximum) for tuition in an approved educational institution. You also can take free courses through the military's own education institute.

You will receive good on-the-job training to prepare you for a skill that will be not only valuable to the service, but also useful to you in civilian life.

The pay is not great, but most single enlisted people find that it's adequate. There are generous fringe benefits, including your pension. Should you wish to leave the military after twenty years, you will be able to retire at 50 percent of your base pay earned just prior to retirement. If you stay in the service, for every year beyond twenty years you will receive an extra 2½ percent of your base pay. This is not something you can do working as a civilian in industry. The retirement plan costs you nothing and is the greatest pension bargain you will find anywhere. Just think, should you decide to retire after twenty years, you will still be comparatively young and can embark on a second career.

Before you start comparing pay scales to those that are paid by private industry, remember that you will also be receiving your board and keep, clothing, and the generous fringe benefits already mentioned.

As a member of the service you are entitled to thirty days of leave annually. When you resign or retire, you will be paid for all the vacation time you have accumulated up to sixty days.

Inexpensive life insurance is available, too. In the event of your death during your service, the government will pay your beneficiaries a death payment. Your dependents will receive monthly checks in amounts depending on your rank.

In many positions, you may request assignments overseas. Since these positions are filled for the most part by volunteers such as yourself, the chances are good that you will have opportunity for foreign travel.

If you are interested in sports, you will find a wide range of athletic and recreational activities in which you may participate.

You may shop at the commissary (also called the PX or post exchange) and save money on almost all items sold there. These post exchanges are operated on a nonprofit basis and admit only service personnel.

Disadvantages of a Military Career

Nothing is perfect. The military has disadvantages. Let's address the most obvious one first.

You could be killed. You could be permanently disfigured. These facts are hammered home anew to the American public when service members return home in wheelchairs or in body bags. This is the biggest risk of all, not only to the infantry but also to members of support units that supply the combat units in time of war.

Aside from the risk of warfare, which every potential service member knows, there are other disadvantages. For example, you may find it difficult to adjust to military life, which is disciplined and regimented. Young people who have been permitted to do pretty much as they wish at home and in the classroom will go from a world of permissiveness to a society of rules and regulations. If this is true for you, the transition may not prove easy.

Some service assignments can be monotonous and boring, whether in the states or abroad. You may be stationed at a post in the desert, where it is extremely hot, and find that there is nothing to do. You might be sent to the land of the midnight sun in an isolated Arctic outpost. This is a chance you must take. Fortunately, there are not too many of these assignments.

Your personal life is subordinated to the military regimen, which must come first. You will probably work an eight-hour day, five days a week. Some assignments must be worked split shifts around the clock, with perhaps extra hours from time to time. You will have to pass grooming inspections. You will have to remember the rules about saluting as well as other special instructions.

If you are enlisted and are married and have a family, your family will have to work to make ends meet. You will not enjoy the luxuries enjoyed by many families in the civilian sector, and you may find yourself living in a relatively small home on base. However, you will be in the company of others like yourself, and you also will find that military families have developed an extensive system of mutual support. No matter where you live or how far you may be from your hometown, you always will have a ready supply of friends who are more than willing to pitch in. And you will do the same for them.

Important Facts About Enlisting

Before you consider enlisting in one of the services, talk to friends who have had military experience and visit one or more recruitment centers to talk with the officers in charge. Read the newspapers to see what units, if any, are being deployed, and if so, what types of duties they are performing. Look at military and civilian-run websites such as Defenselink (www.defenselink.mil) or military.com (www.military.com) to see what types of issues are facing service members. Ask questions.

Although requirements for each service may vary slightly, all branches observe the same general rules. Enlistees must be between seventeen and thirty-five, a U.S. citizen or immigrant alien holding permanent resident status, have no felony record, and have a valid birth certificate. Those who are seventeen must have consent of a parent or a legal guardian before enlisting, and all Air Force personnel must enter active duty before their twenty-eighth birthday. Every applicant must meet certain physical standards such as height, weight, vision, and overall health, as well as pass the written examination known as the Armed Services Vocational Aptitude Battery. High school graduation or its equivalent is a must for certain enlistment options, and single parents are generally not eligible to enlist.

Depending on the terms of an enlistment contract, two to six years may be spent on active duty and the balance in the Reserves. In return for serving satisfactorily for whatever period of time is agreed upon, the service provides numerous benefits. Among these are the generous retirement and pension plans described earlier in this chapter.

In addition to base pay, every soldier or sailor or Marine receives free room and board, occupational training, continuing education, medical and dental care, military clothing allowance, shopping privileges in a military department and supermarket, thirty days of paid vacation each year, and travel opportunities. Those on foreign or hazardous duty, submarine or flight duty, or who are medical officers receive additional allowances. In addition, those who have served at least two years are eligible for various veterans benefits.

A Look at Military Pay

Pay scales are identical for each of the services, so there is no reason to change from one service to another just to increase your earnings. All of the monthly salary figures presented here were in effect as of January 1, 2005. It is possible that since that date Congress has increased all or part of the pay scales. Each service-recruiting officer can give you up-to-date information. It is quite apparent that you must earn promotion to achieve higher earnings. In each of the chapters describing a service, you will find information detailing promotion requirements.

Table 7.1 does not include all ranks or salary information. It merely indicates how salary increases progress.

Table 7.1 Salary Information–Monthly Earnings

Rank	Years of Service			
	1–2	4	10	20
Enlisted Personnel				
E-1*	$1,193.40	$1,193.40		
E-2	$1,337.70	$1,337.70		
E-3	$1,407.00	$1,585.50		
E-4	$1,558.20	$1,814.10		
E-5	$1,700.10	$1,991.10	$2,339.70	
E-6	$1,855.50	$2,218.80	$2,596.20	$2,809.80
E-7	$2,145.00	$2,549.70	$2,891.10	$3,341.70
Warrant Officers**				
W-1	$2,212.80	$2,593.50	$3,039.90	$3,535.80
W-2	$2,505.90	$2,865.30	$3,321.60	$3,843.00
Officers***				
O-1E		$2,848.50	$3,269.40	$5,241.30
O-2E		$3,537.00	$3,918.60	$4,180.20
O-3E		$4,027.20	$4,568.70	$5,241.30
Commissioned Officers				
O-1	$2,264.40	$2,848.50	$2,848.50	$2,848.50
O-2	$2,608.20	$3,537.00	$3,609.90	$3,609.50
O-3	$3,018.90	$4,027.20	$4,568.70	$4,911.30
O-4	$3,433.50	$4,299.00	$5,137.80	$5,241.30

*With less than 4 months service–$1,104.00.
**Rank is higher than that of enlisted personnel but below that of officers.
***With more than 4 years active duty as enlisted or warrant officer.

Why Enlist?

Why would any young man or woman who has completed high school or had further training or college want to become a member of the armed forces? Certainly not because he or she was like so many people who can never keep a job, always come late to work, report sick at the slightest provocation, and think that the only way to make a living would be to join one of the services where a tough sergeant would make him or her get out of bed on time and stick to the job.

Your reasons should be better than these. Perhaps they might resemble the following:

- A desire to serve your country in a useful way.
- An interest in preparing for a career in the military.
- A desire to obtain further education while in the service and later use that training to advance yourself in the military or in civilian employment.
- A quest for a satisfying career with perhaps some adventure thrown in, too. Although a position as an Army truck driver, Marine drafter, or Navy baker sounds hardly adventuresome, each of these positions—and others like them—may involve travel and duty in a part of the world where you can experience both danger and excitement.
- A goal of finding job security for your working years with an assured pension for your old age.
- A desire to work with people whose goals are similar to yours.

There is scarcely a civilian job that is not duplicated in the military services. Therefore, whatever your talents may be, whatever skills you hope to acquire or career you want to pursue, you may be able to fulfill your dreams in one of the services. Remember, should you decide later that military life is not for you, you may be able to apply your service training and experience to a civilian job.

If you are an excellent student and possess well-developed leadership skills, you may qualify for an appointment to one of the military academies. There you can obtain a top-notch education at government expense. Those accepted for a four-year college course must agree to complete a prescribed tour of duty in the service following graduation. This is little enough repayment for a valuable education that is worth—at today's costs—upwards of almost a hundred thousand dollars.

Should your vocational goal be to become a minister, lawyer, dentist, doctor, librarian, or other professional, you will have to study on your own. However, after you have obtained your advanced degree, you might be able to enter the service of your choice in an officer's rank. From there you should be able to carve out a very fine career for yourself.

Whether you should enlist or apply for officer training boils down to what you want to do with your life. If the disciplined military life is agreeable to you, then decide which service is best for you. Before you decide, however, it will be helpful to know how the various services differ in opportunities that will meet your requirements.

The Competitive Services

Each service has certain advantages and disadvantages, but in many respects they are alike. You can obtain training for a career, you may travel, and you will have medical and life insurance, opportunity for further education, and other benefits. Pay scales are comparable, but until you know just what each offers in other ways, you cannot make a good decision.

Thus, if you are a water lover, you would probably want to investigate the Marines, Navy, or Coast Guard. If, on the other hand, airplanes have always been your first love, you might look into the

Air Force. If you have a strong taste for adventure, both the Army and the Marines could fulfill your ambitions, since both of these services see "tip of the spear" action. If American troops must remain in-country following the hot phase of a ground war, the Army traditionally provides the bulk of peacekeeping or occupation forces.

Certain activities are duplicated among all the services. The Air Force is not the only branch flying aircraft. The Army, Coast Guard, Marines, and Navy all have helicopters. The Marine Corps and Navy maintain their own fighter planes. All of the services use motor vehicles of every kind, but all do not sail ships. The Army Corps of Engineers and the Coast Guard, not the Navy, have responsibility over the nation's navigable rivers, harbors, and waterways. On the other hand, all of the services require cooks, bakers, maintenance workers, and clerical staffs. They also need doctors, dentists, engineers, librarians, chaplains, and hundreds of other kinds of trained specialists.

If you are wise you will investigate each branch. You can do this by rereading the previous chapters carefully, taking time to note the service differences. Be sure you know the mission of each and where you might best fit in. Then you can decide whether you honestly feel that enlisting or entering an officer training program would prove a worthwhile investment of time for you—and also for the government.

8

EDUCATION FOR THE MILITARY

A SAD FACT of life today is the high cost of a four-year college education. If you attend an elite school, you could spend $130,000 or more for a four-year stay. Less prestigious institutions also command high fees. Even state universities are expensive. Although a wide range of scholarships and other financial aid programs are available, many young people choose to pursue the two-year diplomas that are offered by more affordable community colleges or vocational/technical schools.

Uncle Sam offers an alternative. Each year, select applicants earn slots at one of the government's four-year military academies—at absolutely no cost to the student. A diploma from any one of these prestigious universities virtually guarantees a successful military or subsequent civilian career.

These academy educations are worth about $100,000 each. This is the approximate cost of educating each graduate of the four military service academies, which prepare officers for the armed services. There is a catch, of course. To earn acceptance at one of these schools, you must be an outstanding and well-rounded student. Before applying, you must ask yourself some very direct questions. Do you have exceptionally good grades in school? Did you participate in extracurricular activities? Are you in excellent physical condition? Would you agree to remain with the service for at least five years after graduation from a military academy? And, perhaps most important, do you have the determination to stick it out through four tough years of military training and academic scholarship?

The Four Academies

The Air Force, Army, Navy, and Coast Guard all operate academies. These are located, respectively, in Colorado Springs, Colorado; West Point, New York; Annapolis, Maryland; and New London, Connecticut. Each university has a four-year program leading to a Bachelor of Science degree. Each is open to men and women. Student cadets and midshipmen receive tuition, room and board, and medical care, plus a monthly allowance for incidental expenses. Upon graduation, students are awarded commissions for active periods of at least five years. Air force graduates who take pilot training after graduation must serve eight years.

Thumbnail Sketches

The United States Military Academy, established in 1802, was originally a school for Army engineers who were stationed at West Point. As it became evident that there would be war with England again, Congress expanded the academy and enlarged the corps of engineers. Subsequently, the academy became famous for the civil engineers it trained. After the Civil War, the school dissolved its tie with the corps of engineers. Today, by law, the number of cadets is set at 4,417—about 10 percent of whom are women. It is considered one of the leading institutions of higher education in the nation.

The Naval Academy at Annapolis trains young men and women to be officers of the Navy and the Marine Corps. Founded in 1845 by Secretary of the Navy George Bancroft, the campus has always been at Annapolis except during the Civil War, when it was moved to Newport, Rhode Island. The four-year school offers general studies as well as scientific and technical courses on naval subjects, along with practical experiences on seagoing cruises.

The next academy to be authorized was that of the United States Coast Guard in 1877. It gave cadets an academic and military education. It also offered practical training at sea prior to receiving an officer's commission. The academy is the only one for which admission is by nationwide competition based on how well you place on the Scholastic Aptitude Test (SAT) and American College Test (ACT), plus your class ranking and leadership qualities. Deadline for applications is December 15. Qualifying SAT or ACT examinations must be taken prior to or during December. This school offers a choice of nine majors, which lead to a B.S. in the fields of marine engineering, ocean engineering, electrical engineering, civil engineering, marine science, mathematical science, physical sciences, management, and government. Of the three thousand applications received each year, half are thrown out because they are not filled out properly, even though most of them had a chance of meeting minimum standards. Only three hundred are accepted.

The youngest of the service academies, the Air Force Academy, is located in Colorado Springs, Colorado. Congress authorized establishment of the Air Force Academy on April 1, 1954. The first officers were commissioned on June 3, 1959. Enrollment is limited to 4,546. Of that number, 15 percent are ethnic minorities and 12 percent are women. The academy is well known for its science and engineering programs. The school also offers majors in the humanities and social sciences, preparing cadets for Air Force career fields other than engineering.

Life at the Coast Guard Academy

Academy life is highly disciplined. All cadets are subject to the Uniform Code of Military Justice. Cadets live under an administrative disciplinary system that is prescribed in cadet regulations. New cadets come under the "Fourth Class System" for their training and indoctrinating. This means that they take orders from upperclassmen as well as commissioned officers. A number of rules are established for the behavior of fourth classmen, or "swabs," to help make the transition from civilian to military life. This system is designed to teach discipline, respect for authority, and self-control. Each class is given increased authority annually until one day a former member of the fourth class will be a regimental commander.

Have you wondered what a typical day might be like in a military academy? Here is how the Coast Guard described its routine:

All cadets live on campus at the academy. Each cadet shares a room that is neatly furnished with everything required for comfortable living and studying.

There are daily inspections to make sure the rooms are clean and orderly. Cadets follow a carefully planned routine of activities.

A typical day begins at 6:10 A.M. when reveille is sounded. The cadet is awakened and begins preparation for the day. Morning classes start at 7:50 and go until 11:40. Personnel inspection is held before lunch on Monday, Wednesday, and Friday. Lunch is at noon, followed by afternoon classes from 12:45 until 3:35. The hours between 3:35 and 6:30 P.M. are devoted to intramural or varsity sports, extracurricular activities, or extra classes if cadets need individual help.

Dinner is at 6:30. From 7:00 to 8:00 cadets may work on extracurricular activities or begin their studies. Study time is from 7:00 to 10:00. Taps mark the end of the day at 10:15. Study is permitted until midnight.

It's a full life, as you can see. It's one reason why Coast Guard officers are tough, disciplined, exacting leaders.

On Friday afternoons in the fall and spring there are formal regimental parades. Saturday mornings are devoted to professional training. Liberty, which means permission to leave the Academy grounds, is granted on Saturday afternoons and evenings and again on Sundays. Senior upperclassmen are also given liberty on Wednesday and all upperclassmen on Friday afternoons at 4:00 P.M.

Here is how you may spend your summers while at the Coast Guard Academy:

After a few weeks' leave, your summers will be largely devoted to professional training. The first summer is mostly spent at the Academy, where the emphasis is on orientation, physical fitness, and competitive sports. The big highlight of the summer is a one-week cruise aboard the *Eagle*, the Coast Guard's three-masted bark.

A long cruise occupies most of the second summer aboard Coast Guard cutters or the *Eagle*. Your third summer is spent learning seamanship, navigation, and firefighting. Then there are two weeks learning the theories and operation of aircraft.

The final summer is usually spent on cruise to foreign ports with additional time spent in actual Coast Guard operations in special fields of interest.

How to Apply

If you are interested in obtaining an education at one of the academies, the first step is to apply for a nomination (except when applying to the Coast Guard Academy, where entrance is based on nationwide competition). To obtain a nomination, write to your congressional representative in Washington, DC. You can find his or her name online at www.house.gov or at www. senate.gov. In your letter to the representative, you should state which academy or academies you are interested in attending. You also should ask for information about securing a nomination. At the same time, write to the academy and request a precandidate questionnaire.

Each member of Congress may have five of his or her constituents at each of the academies and may nominate as many as ten applicants for each vacancy. You should apply for a congressional nomination during the spring of your junior year in high school. Some members of Congress will accept requests for nominations as late as November or early December of your senior year, but it is wiser to apply early.

Although the nomination process varies slightly in each service, nominations may be available if one of your parents is a career member of the military services, is on active duty and has served for at least eight years, is retired from active duty, or is a deceased retired veteran. If your parent was service connected or was a federally employed civilian who is in a missing or captured status, you may request a nomination under this category. Children of Medal of Honor recipients may seek separate appointments to the academy of their choice without regard to vacancies, provided they meet minimum qualifying standards.

Appointments may be made also for residents of American Samoa by the governor; for residents of the Virgin Islands, Guam, and the

District of Columbia by their delegates to Congress; and for residents of Puerto Rico by the governor and resident commissioner.

Remember that if you obtain this free education, you will have a five-year service obligation following graduation.

For further information contact: Director of Cadet Admissions, HQ USAFA/RRS, 2304 Cadet Drive, Suite 200, U.S. Air Force Academy, Colorado Springs, Colorado 80840-5025, www.acade myadmissions.com or www.usafa.af.mil; Office of Admission, U.S. Military Academy, West Point, New York 10996, www.asma.edu; Director of Candidate Guidance, U.S. Naval Academy, Annapolis, Maryland 21402, www.usna.edu; Director of Admissions, U.S. Coast Guard Academy, New London, Connecticut 06320-4195, www.cga.edu.

Mention should also be made of the United States Merchant Marine Academy, which trains officers who operate the merchant marine ships of our country. Graduates of this school also serve in such other capacities as ship designers (naval architects), maritime lawyers, port engineers, shipping-company executives, naval officers, Coast Guard officers, and oceanographers.

The Merchant Marine Academy, located at Kings Point, New York, was established in 1943 under the Maritime Administration, which is now under the Department of Transportation. The academy ranks as one of the foremost institutions in the field of maritime education. The government provides all midshipmen a four-year scholarship covering tuition, room, and board.

Military Prep Schools

Three military services have operated preparatory schools to help young people meet the very high admission standards of the military academies. These schools work to strengthen students' backgrounds in English, mathematics, and science as a foundation for entrance into one of the service academies.

In the case of the Army's Fort Monmouth school, the ten-month course starts in August of each year and ends on June 1 of the following year. Applicants must be at least seventeen and not more than twenty-one years of age on July 1 of the year of entrance; a United States citizen, unmarried, with no dependents; in good health; and a high school graduate or the equivalent.

In the Army's school, each weekday starts promptly at 5:45 A.M. and ends at 11:00 P.M. Studies include two one-hour sessions in English and two in mathematics each day, as well as a study period from 8:00 until 11:00 at night. There also is time for sports and physical training. While in school, the students become members of the Army's enlisted reserve. They receive pay in accordance with their rank.

Students live in dormitory double-bunk rooms. Discipline is strict. The school offers a library, video games, television, pinball machines, and a gym with exercise machines and weightlifting equipment for recreation. Permission is granted for weekends off the post if a student is in good academic standing.

The Air Force starts its ten-month course in July and ends classes in May. The Naval Academy preparatory school provides a nine-month course that runs from mid-August to late May.

In the case of the Navy's school, every application for appointment to the Naval Academy is also considered an application for the preparatory school; no separate application is possible. If you are not accepted for the Naval Academy, it is possible you may be offered an appointment to the preparatory school. The Coast Guard Academy also selects its students for assignment to the Naval Academy preparatory school in a similar way. If you are accepted for the preparatory school, you will be enlisted in the armed forces and be paid according to the pay grade for that position. You only need pay for your personal expenses.

For further information, write the following: Director of Cadet Admissions, USAF Academy, Colorado Springs, Colorado 80840; Commandant, U.S. Military Academy Preparatory School, Attention MAPS-AD-A, Ft. Monmouth, New Jersey 07703; Director of Candidate Guidance, U.S. Naval Academy, Annapolis, Maryland 21401.

Reserve Officer Training Corps

If you are not interested in trying for one of the military academies, it is possible you still might qualify for financial assistance to pay most or part of your college education. You may be able to achieve this via the ROTC scholarship program or through one of the other plans designed to help young men and women obtain an education while preparing for military service. The provisions of these aid plans vary somewhat from service to service and also are subject to change without notice. Therefore, to avoid giving misleading information, we suggest that if you are seeking help to go to college and are ready to serve in the military for several years after you complete your education, you should take a number of steps. They include the following:

1. Select the service or services that interest you.
2. Think carefully about your career goals. Bear in mind what each service does and know that if you are accepted, you will have a job that could become your lifetime career.
3. Prepare to explain and discuss your educational and vocational plans and expectations.

4. Contact the local recruiting office listed in your telephone book under United States Government, or write to one of the offices listed below.

5. Talk with a recruiter and learn more about the opportunities available to you. If necessary, be ready to modify your plans to fit your educational goals.

Even if you are already in college, it is not too late to look into the possibility of a ROTC or other financial aid plan. The important thing is not to put it off but to investigate now, because it takes time to file applications, take examinations, and process all of the required documents.

ROTC programs are not available at all colleges. Additionally, some schools have only a two-year program; others offer both two- and four-year programs. Each of the services will send you a list of colleges that offer their ROTC programs, plus information about admissions standards. Standards usually include passing the service physical examination and achieving a minimum grade on the SAT or ACT examination, as well as on the officers' qualification tests. Obviously, you must maintain certain grade averages while in college.

For the latest information about ROTC and how you might best fit into the program, contact the nearest recruiting officer of the Air Force, Army, Navy, or Marines, or write or call the following:

- **Air Force.** USAF Recruiting Service, Randolph AFB, Texas 78150-4527
- **Army.** U.S. Army Recruiting Command, Ft. Knox, Kentucky 40121-2726

- **Navy and Marines.** Call the Navy's toll-free information number, (800) 424-8883, and ask for a referral to the nearest officer programs officer.

A final suggestion: Your guidance counseling office or high school library may have the latest ROTC literature available for you to consult or borrow.

Officer Candidate Training Schools

If you are in college and are not interested in taking ROTC, or if it is too late to enroll, it is still possible to enter one of the services as an officer. After graduation from college you can apply for officer candidate training. The general requirements are a degree from an accredited institution, United States citizenship, and the ability to pass the service physical examination. Age limits are generally from eighteen to twenty-nine, but waivers may be granted for those who are older. Applicants for flight training may find a slightly lower age limit.

As mentioned elsewhere, direct appointments are available to professionals in the medical or health science fields, attorneys, chaplains, and engineers, as well as certain other scientifically or professionally trained personnel.

9

ARMED FORCES
NONMILITARY CAREERS

DID YOU KNOW that nearly seven hundred thousand men and women work in civilian positions for the Department of Defense? The military employs men and women in almost every kind of federal occupation that exists. If you have poor eyesight, a heart murmur, a perforated eardrum, or other physical problem, you probably will be unable to pass the physical examination when you apply for enlistment or officer candidate training. There is, however, another route to a career in the military: through the federal government's civil service system.

Civilian Jobs in the Armed Forces

Most of the occupations are administered under the federal civil service system. This means that when you apply for a particular opening, you must compete with other applicants. You will be evaluated by the Office of Personnel Management (formerly called the Civil Service Commission) or the service for which you hope to work.

The Office of Personnel Management (OPM) acts as a clearing agency for all other government agencies and the armed services. As civilian vacancies occur, the various agencies request the names of people qualified to fill the positions. The best-qualified applicants' names are referred from OPM lists, and these are considered for the openings.

Whether you will be hired depends on your qualifications and the number of applicants for the same job or jobs. It also depends on the salary level you say you will accept and on how quickly the jobs become vacant. If enough qualified applicants have had their names accepted for the lists, the OPM stops accepting any more names. However, you should bear in mind that although there might be sufficient applicants in one location, there might be openings in another area for the same type of job. If you have the option to relocate, it might be worth considering such a position.

From time to time the OPM issues lists of job openings within the federal government, including the dates of competitive examinations. Information about these and other job openings is available at local offices of the OPM and usually at state employment security offices. The best way to proceed is to contact one of the federal job information and testing centers listed in many telephone books under United States Government. If there is no listing in your telephone book, contact the nearest state employment security office, which should have the information. Employment security offices are located throughout most states. If you cannot find the address in your phone book, check Internet search services or ask your librarian or postmaster to help you.

To qualify for most federal jobs, you must have the education or experience specified for the grade level or job you want. Some jobs do not have rigid requirements regarding education and experience. For these you need only provide information about yourself. Each job description lists the particular requirements you will need.

Another way to learn about possible civilian openings is to contact the public information office of the Department of Defense service in which you want to work. For your convenience, they are listed here:

- **Department of Defense.** Chief Staffing and Support Programs, The Pentagon, Washington, DC 20301
- **Department of the Air Force.** Public Affairs Office, Department of the Air Force, The Pentagon, Washington, DC 20330-1670; (800) 423-USAR
- **Department of the Army.** For employment in the Washington, DC area, Personnel and Employment Service— Washington, Room 3D727, The Pentagon, Washington, DC 20310-6800. For employment outside Washington, write or apply directly to the army installation where employment is desired, Attention: Civilian Personnel Office. For employment overseas, U.S. Army Personnel Center, Attention: PECC-CSS, Hoffman II Building, 200 Stovall Street, Alexandria, Virginia 22332-0300; (800) USA-ARMY
- **Department of the Navy.** Navy Recruiting Command, Capital Region, 801 North Randolph Street, Arlington, Virginia 22203-1991; (800) 424-8883
- **Marine Corps.** Commandant of the Marine Corps, Headquarters, U.S. Marine Corps, Washington, DC 20380-0001; (800) MARINES

- **Coast Guard.** Since this service is a division of the Department of Transportation, openings are best located through the federal job information centers, or consult your state Employment Security Department listed in the white pages of your telephone directory.

The Veterans Administration

The Veterans Administration (VA) is a huge organization that administers benefits to the men and women who have served in the armed forces. It also operates the nation's largest health care delivery system. It has an extensive network of hospitals and outpatient clinics. The VA provides hospitalization and outpatient dental and medical care to all eligible veterans. Most hospitals are of the general medical and surgical type, but there is also some provision for psychiatric care.

There is at least one regional (benefits) office in each state and Puerto Rico. Here eligible veterans and their dependents may obtain benefits such as compensation and pensions for disability or death, loan guaranties for homes, job training, educational assistance under the GI bill, insurance, and other related services.

Known as the federal government's most automated agency, the VA maintains automated data processing centers to do the record keeping for the various benefits, medical, and administrative programs of this vast organization. The computers operate seven days a week, twenty-four hours a day.

In addition, the VA operates and maintains more than one hundred national cemeteries throughout the country. Most are in or near small cities and towns in rural areas; some are located adjacent to large urban areas.

With its many hospitals, the VA requires large numbers of support personnel, principally housekeeping aides and food-service workers. Housekeeping aides keep the hospitals sparkling clean. Aides' duties include cleaning rooms and corridors, stripping and waxing floors, cleaning carpets, hanging curtains and draperies, delivering supplies to the wards, and operating the various machines used in this work. These types of aides do not work directly with patients but are likely to come in contact with sick or severely wounded soldiers and veterans.

The food-service workers help prepare the meals, make salads and desserts, assemble food on the trays, and deliver them to the patients. They also operate dishwashing machines and do other jobs associated with preparing meals and cleaning dishes, silverware, pots, and pans. At the starting levels for housekeeping aides and food-service workers, there are no education or experience requirements.

Maintenance of the large hospitals calls for a variety of skilled craftsmen such as carpenters, plumbers, steamfitters, electricians, masons, painters, and air-conditioning and refrigeration repairers. In addition to these trained specialists, the hospital staffs include laborers, gardeners, cemetery caretakers, medical equipment repairers, motor vehicle operators, warehouse employees, and many other specialists. For most of the unskilled jobs that involve helping the craft employees such as carpenters, electricians, or plumbers, there are no educational requirements. Evidence that you have potential to learn and advance is important. To qualify for a journeyman or craft position, you must show that you can perform that particular skill.

Most of the positions mentioned here are in VA health care facilities. Only a few are in the regional offices, data processing centers, or national cemeteries. To learn about openings, contact the nearest federal job information center or the personnel office of the VA nearest you. Also, if you live near a VA hospital or office (consult your telephone book under United States Government—Veterans Administration), visit the personnel office for information and an interview.

Professionally trained men and women will find good career opportunities with the VA. Some of the many professional job titles for which there are frequent openings include architects, engineers, dietitians, dentists, doctors, audiologists and speech pathologists, registered and practical nurses, and medical technologists.

10

What's Your Decision?

CHOOSING A CAREER is not an easy task whether you are seventeen, twenty-one, or thirty. Many young people have no real idea what they want to do. They may have to take several jobs before they learn their true career interest. The military is one employer that builds in a tryout period, so that you sign on to work for a relatively short amount of time, during which you will learn more about yourself and your career goals. Besides, you won't find another job opportunity where you can earn while you learn—not a bad way to start!

If you do decide to join the military, you are faced with a number of choices. Which service do you prefer? Do you intend to enlist, apply for officer training, or seek a civil service appointment? What type of job do you want? Something that would put you on the front lines of our nation's defense; or a support position not likely to place you in the line of fire?

These are weighty questions that should not be answered hastily. You may want to discuss them with your parents, guidance counselor, clergyperson, or other adults whose judgment you respect. By all means, talk with the recruiting officer of the service or services that interest you; but bear in mind that while he or she will answer your questions honestly, the recruiter's job is to recruit.

It is not too early to start planning for your future. If you are in high school or college, the best ways to prepare are to take the courses that will give you the required background for what you want to do. Then you must work hard to achieve the best grades you can. Your school or college record is most important to your future, be it in military or civilian careers.

It's up to you, and you alone, to decide what you will do with your life. Remember, if you choose the military route to a career, your decision is neither irreversible nor wasteful. If the military is not for you, then you can serve out your term and return to civilian life. Or, if you and the military are a good match, you can extend your original service term. The choice to join the military comes with potential hazards and unknowns. It is also a noble choice that benefits both the individual and the nation.

Navy Occupational Specialties

The following data present a sample of some typical occupational specialties. For each career field, information is listed about duties and responsibilities, qualifications, and examples of civilian jobs.

Fire Control

- Operates, tests, maintains, and repairs weapons control systems and telemetering equipment used to compute and resolve factors that influence accuracy of torpedoes and missiles.
- Is able to perform fine, detailed work. Has extensive training in mathematics, electronics, electricity, and mechanics.
- Job titles include radar or electronics technician, test range tracker, instrument repairer, and electrician.

Sonar

- Operates underwater detection and attack apparatus; obtains and interprets information for tactical purposes; maintains and repairs electronic underwater sound-detection equipment.
- Possesses normal hearing and clear speaking voice; background in algebra, geometry, physics, electricity, and shop work is desirable as is an aptitude for electrical and mechanical work.
- Job titles include oil-well sounding-device operator, radio operator, inspector or electronic assemblies, electronic technician, electrical repairer, and fire control mechanic.

Aviation (Structural)

- Maintains and repairs aircraft, airframe, structural components, hydraulic controls, utility systems, and egress systems.
- Possesses a high degree of mechanical aptitude; a background in metal shop, algebra, plane geometry, and physics and experience in automobile body work is helpful.
- Job titles include welder, sheet-metal repairer, hydraulics technician, radiographer, and aircraft plumbing systems mechanic.

Engine

- Operates, services, and repairs internal combustion engines, ship propulsion machinery, refrigeration and air-

conditioning systems, air compressors, and related electrohydraulic equipment.
- Demonstrates clear speech, physical stamina, and manual dexterity; knowledge of arithmetic and internal combustion engines is desirable.
- Job titles include diesel plant engine operator, diesel mechanic, automobile engine mechanic, marine engine machinist, stationary engineer, fuel-system maintenance worker, and power-plant operator.

Machinery and Equipment

- Operates, maintains, and repairs steam turbines and reduction gears used for ship's propulsion and auxiliary equipment such as turbo generators, pumps, refrigeration/air conditioning, and laundry equipment.
- Demonstrates aptitude for mechanical work, physical stamina, and ability to work well with others; background in practical or shop mathematics, machine shop, electricity, and physics is valuable.
- Job titles include power-plant operator, oxygen-plant operator, marine mechanic, diesel mechanic, stationary engineer/mechanic, and refrigeration mechanic.

Construction (Electrical)

- Installs, operates, maintains, and repairs electrical generating and distribution systems, transformers, switchboards, motors, and controllers.

- Demonstrates interest in mechanical and electrical work; can work aloft; background in electricity, shop mathematics, and physics is helpful.
- Job titles include powerhouse or construction electrician, electrical and telephone repairer, power-plant operator, and diesel-plant operator.

Dental

- Assists dental officers, administers dental hygiene, makes dental X-rays, and performs administrative duties. Some may qualify in dental prosthetical laboratory techniques and maintenance and repair of dental equipment.
- Possesses scientific background or interests, normal color vision, competence with tools, good communication skills, and ability to perform repetitive tasks without losing interest.
- Job titles include dental assistant, dental records clerk, dental laboratory technician, dental X-ray technician, dental hygienist, dental equipment repairer/technical representatives.

Illustration/Drafting

- Designs, sketches, does layouts, and makes signs, charts, and training aids; operates visual presentation equipment; uses art media, computer reproduction systems, and graphic arts equipment.

- Has previous experience as draftsperson, tracer, or surveyor; is creative, possesses manual dexterity, and is competent in math; background in art, mechanical drawing, and blueprint reading is valuable.
- Job titles include structural draftsperson, technical illustrator, specification writer, electrical draftsperson, and graphic artist.

Music

- Provides music for military ceremonies, religious services, concerts, parades, and various recreational activities; plays one or more musical instruments.
- Demonstrates proficiency on standard band or orchestral instruments.
- Job titles include music teacher, instrument musician, orchestra leader, music arranger, instrument repairer, and music librarian.

Religious Program

- Supports chaplains of all faiths and religious activities of the command; assists in management and development of the command's religious programs and determinations of resources; maintains records of various funds, ecclesiastical documents, and references.

- Can type, express ideas, do detailed work, and keep accurate records; has good moral character, interest in people, initiative, and writing skills.
- Job titles include church business administrator, religious facilities manager, and administrative assistant.

Store

- Orders, receives, stores, inventories, and issues clothing, foodstuffs, mechanical equipment, and general supplies.
- Possesses skills in typing, bookkeeping, accounting, commercial math, general business studies, and English.
- Job titles include sales or shipping clerk, warehouse worker, buyer, invoice control clerk, purchasing agent, travel clerk, accounting clerk, bookkeeper, and stock control clerk.

Building

- Constructs, maintains, and repairs wood, concrete, and masonry structures; erects and repairs waterfront structures.
- Demonstrates high mechanical aptitude; background in carpentry and shop mathematics as well as experience with hand and power tools is valuable.
- Job titles include plasterer, roofer, mason, painter, construction worker, carpenter, and estimator.

Optical Equipment

- Maintains scientifically accurate optical tools used for visual aids and required for navigation and weapons systems. Manufactures optical parts such as lens cells.
- Demonstrates orientation toward fine tools and precision equipment and machinery; possesses manual dexterity and resourcefulness; background in physics, shop math, and machine shop/tools is helpful.
- Job titles include precision instrument technician, toolmaker, locksmith, instrument mechanic, optical instrument assembler, and camera repairer.

Ship Duty

- Performs navigation of ships, steering, lookout supervision, shop control, bridge-watch duties, visual communication, and maintenance of navigational aids.
- Has good vision and hearing and ability to express self clearly in writing and speaking; background in geometry and physics is helpful.
- Job titles include barge, motorboat, yacht captain, quartermaster, and harbor pilot aboard merchant ships.

Appendix B

Marine Corps Occupational Specialties

THE FOLLOWING DATA present a sample of some typical occupational specialties. For each career field, information is listed about duties and responsibilities, qualifications, and examples of civilian jobs.

Infantry

- Performs as rifleman, machine gunner, or grenadier infantry unit leader; supervises training and operations of infantry units.
- Demonstrates good verbal and mathematical reasoning; has good vision and stamina; possesses general mathematics, mechanical drafting, geography, and mechanical drawing skills.

- Job titles include firearms assembler, gunsmith, policeman, immigration inspector, and plant security policeman.

Motor Transport

- Performs auto mechanics and body repair, motor vehicle, and amphibian truck operations.
- Demonstrates abilities in automotive mechanics, machine shop, electricity, and reading blueprints.
- Job titles include automobile mechanic, electrical systems repairer, truck driver, motor vehicle dispatcher, and motor transport.

Avionics

- Installs and repairs aircraft electrical, communications/navigation, and fire control equipment and air-launched guided missiles; serves as electrician and instrument repairer.
- Demonstrates abilities in mathematics; shop course in electricity, hydraulics, and electronics useful.
- Job titles include radio and TV or electrical instrument repairer; communications, electrical, or electronics engineer; and radio operator.

Data/Communications Maintenance

- Installs, inspects, and repairs telephone, teletype, and cryptographic equipment and cables; calibrates precision electronic, mechanical, dimensional, and optical test instruments.

- Mathematics, electricity, and blueprint reading courses are helpful.
- Job titles include telephone installer and troubleshooter, radio repairer, cable splicer, and office machine serviceperson.

Auditing, Finance, and Accounting

- Prepares and audits personnel pay records, processes public vouchers, and administers and audits unit fiscal accounts.
- Possesses computational work skills and attention to detail; skills in typing, bookkeeping, office machines, and mathematics are useful.
- Job titles include payroll or cost clerk, bookkeeper, cashier, bank teller, accounting and audit clerk, and accountant.

Food Service

- Performs as cook, baker, or meat cutter.
- Hygiene, biology, chemistry, home economics, and bookkeeping courses are useful.
- Job titles include cook, chef, baker, meat cutter or butcher, caterer, executive chef, dietician, and restaurant manager.

Music

- Performs in Marine Corps Band, unit bands, and Drum and Bugle Corps; repairs musical instruments.
- Has music experience as a member of a high school band or orchestra.

- Job titles include musician, music librarian, music teacher, bandmaster, orchestra or music director, and musical instrument repairer.

Transportation

- Handles cargo and transacts business or freight shipping and receiving and passenger transportation.
- Has some skills in typing, bookkeeping, business, arithmetic, office machine operation, and commercial subjects.
- Job titles include shipping clerk, cargo handler, freight traffic clerk, passenger and railroad station agent.

Air Traffic Control and Enlisted Flight Crew/ Air Support/Anti-Warfare

- Operates airfield control tower and radio-radar air-traffic control systems; serves as navigator, radio and radar operator.
- Possesses a clear speaking voice, good hearing, and better-than-average eyesight; has a background in mathematics and electricity; experience as a ham radio operator is helpful.
- Job titles include airport control tower or flight radio operator, navigator, truck operator, and radio or television studio engineer.

Data Systems

- Operates and programs data processing equipment.

- Demonstrates clerical aptitude, manual dexterity and hand-eye coordination, and skills in mathematics, accounting, and English.
- Job titles include computer operator or programmer and data control coordinator.

Intelligence

- Collects, records, evaluates, and interprets information; makes detailed study of aerial photographs; conducts interrogations in foreign languages; translates written material; and interprets conversations.
- Has some background in geography, history, government, economics, English, foreign languages, typing, mechanical drafting, and mathematics.
- Job titles include investigator, research worker, intelligence analyst (government), map drafter, cartographic aide, and records analyst.

Nuclear, Biological, and Chemical

- Performs routine duties to apply detection, emergency, and decontamination measures to gassed or radioactive areas. Inspects and performs preventive maintenance on chemical warfare protection equipment.
- Must not have any known hypersensitivity to the wearing of protective clothing; be emotionally stable; biology and chemistry background is beneficial.

- Job titles include laboratory assistant (nuclear, biological, or chemical), exterminator, and decontaminator.

Utilities

- Installs, operates, and maintains electrical, water supply, heating, plumbing, sewage, refrigeration, hygiene, and air-conditioning equipment.
- Demonstrates good mechanical aptitude and manual dexterity; vocational school shop course in industrial arts and crafts is beneficial.
- Job titles include electrician, plumber, steam fitter, refrigeration mechanic, electric motor repairer, and stationary engineer.

Weather Service

- Collects, records, and analyzes meteorological data; makes visual and instrumental observations.
- Must have visual acuity correctable to 20/20 and normal color perception; background in mathematics, meteorology, and astronomy is helpful.
- Job titles include meteorologist and weather forecaster/observer.

Appendix C

Army Occupational Specialties

THE FOLLOWING DATA present a sample of some typical occupational specialties. For each career field, information is listed about duties and responsibilities, qualifications, and examples of civilian jobs.

Armor

- Operates and maintains heavy equipment over rough terrain. Serves as a member of reconnaissance, security, or special operations force. Interprets maps and operational data.
- Demonstrates a high degree of ability in leadership, communications, mathematics, and mechanical maintenance. Is physically fit.

- Job titles include supervisor, heavy equipment operator or repairer, truck mechanic, and armament machinist.

Field Artillery

- Serves or supervises in the operation/intelligence, fire support, and target acquisition activities of a highly specialized organization. Operates unique rocket launching computers that assist cannons and rockets in obtaining maximum accuracy. Operates and maintains radar as well as meteorological and survey equipment.
- Demonstrates good mathematical reasoning, abilities in mechanical maintenance, meteorology, and communications. Is physically fit.
- Job titles include supervisor, surveyor, topographical drafter, cartographer, meteorologist, and radio operator.

Aircraft Maintenance

- Performs the mechanical functions of maintenance, repair, and modification of helicopters and turboprop engine aircraft.
- Demonstrates considerable mechanical or electrical aptitude and manual dexterity; background in shop mathematics and physics is desirable.
- Job titles include aircraft mechanic and plane inspector.

Finance and Accounting

- Maintains pay records for military personnel; prepares vouchers for payment; prepares reports; disburses funds; accounts for funds to include budgeting, allocation, and auditing; compiles and analyzes statistical data; and prepares cost analysis records.
- Demonstrates dexterity in the operation of business machines. Typing, mathematics, statistics, and basic principles of accounting are desirable and high administrative aptitude is mandatory.
- Job titles include paymaster, cashier, statistical or audit clerk, accountant, budget clerk, and bookkeeper.

Military Police

- Enforces military regulations; protects facilities, roads, designated sensitive areas, and personnel; controls traffic movement; guards military prisoners and enemy prisoners of war.
- Possesses sociology background and demonstrates leadership in athletics and other group work.
- Job titles include police officer, plant guard, detective, investigator, crime detection laboratory assistant, and ballistics expert.

Petroleum

- Receives, stores, preserves, and distributes bulk-packaged petroleum products; performs standard physical and

chemical tests of petroleum products; is involved in storage and distribution of purified water.
- Has a background in hygiene, biology, physics, chemistry, and mathematics.
- Job titles include biological laboratory assistant, petroleum tester, and chemical laboratory assistant.

Transportation

- Operates and performs preventive maintenance on personnel, light, medium, and heavy cargo vehicles; operates and maintains marine harbor craft; performs as air traffic controller.
- Has good mechanical aptitude, manual dexterity, hand-eye coordination, FAA certification for air traffic control, and license for vehicle operation.
- Job titles include truck driver and FAA air traffic controller.

Automatic Data Processing

- Operates a variety of electrical accounting and automatic data processing equipment to produce personnel, supply, fiscal, medical, intelligence, and other reports.
- Possesses good reasoning and verbal ability, clerical aptitude, manual dexterity, and hand-eye coordination. Has knowledge of typing and office machines.

- Job titles include coding clerk, keypunch operator, computer and sorting machine operator, and machine records unit supervisor.

Electronic Warfare Cryptologic Operations

- Collects and analyzes electromagnetic transmissions in fixed or mobile operations.
- Possesses good verbal and reasoning ability, perceptual speed, and hearing and visual acuity.
- Job titles include radio and telegraph operator, navigator, intelligence research analyst, statistician, and signal collection technician.

General Engineering

- Provides utilities and engineering services such as electric power production, building and roadway construction and maintenance, salvage activities, airstrip construction, firefighting, and crash rescue operations.
- Possesses good mechanical aptitude, emotional stability, and ability to visualize spatial relationships. Is skilled in carpentry, woodworking, or mechanical drawing.
- Job titles include carpenter, construction equipment operator, electrician, firefighter, driver, plumber, welder, and bricklayer.

Military Intelligence

- Gathers, translates, correlates, and interprets information, including imagery, associated with military plans and operations.
- Demonstrates skill in English composition, typing, foreign languages, mathematics, and geography.
- Job titles include investigator, interpreter, records analyst, research worker, and intelligence analyst (government).

Appendix D

Air Force Occupational Specialties

THE FOLLOWING DATA present a sample of some typical occupational specialties. For each career field, information is listed about duties and responsibilities, qualifications, and examples of civilian jobs.

Aircraft Maintenance

- Performs the mechanical functions of maintenance, repair, and modification of helicopters, turboprop, reciprocation engine, and jet aircraft.
- Possesses considerable mechanical or electrical aptitude and manual dexterity; background in physics, hydraulics, electronics, mathematics, and mechanics is desirable.
- Job titles include aircraft mechanic and airframe inspector.

Vehicle Maintenance

- Overhauls and maintains powered ground vehicles and mechanical equipment for transporting personnel and supplies.
- Background in machine shop, mathematics, and training in the use of tools and blueprints is helpful.
- Job titles include automobile accessories installer; automobile and truck mechanic.

Sanitation

- Operates and maintains water and waste-processing plant systems and equipment and performs pest and rodent control functions.
- Background in physics, biology, chemistry, and reading blueprints is desirable.
- Job titles include purification plant operator, sanitary inspector, exterminator, and entomologist.

Security

- Provides security for classified information and material, enforces law and order, controls traffic, protects lives and property, organizes as local ground-defense force.
- Has good physical condition, vision, and hearing; background in civics and social sciences is desirable.
- Job titles include guard, police inspector, police officer, and superintendent of police.

Fuels

- Receives, stores, dispenses, tests, and inspects propellants, petroleum fuels, and products.
- Background in chemistry, math, and general science is desirable.
- Job titles include petroleum industry supervisor and bulk plant manager.

Accounting, Finance, and Auditing

- Prepares documents required to account for and disburse funds, including budgeting, allocation, disbursing, auditing, and preparing cost-analysis records.
- Can operate business machines and demonstrates high administrative aptitude; background in typing, mathematics, statistics, and accounting is desirable.
- Job titles include public accountant, auditor, bookkeeper, budget clerk, and paymaster.

Band

- Plays musical instruments or sings in concert bands and orchestras, repairs and maintains instruments, performs as drum major, arranges music, and maintains music libraries.
- Knowledge of elementary theory of music and orchestration is desirable.
- Job titles include orchestrator, music librarian, music teacher, and instrumental musician.

Dental

- Operates dental facilities and provides paraprofessional dental care and preventive dental services, treats oral tissues, and fabricates prosthetic devices.
- Demonstrates knowledge of oral and dentin anatomy, biology, and chemistry.
- Job titles include dental hygienist and dental assistant.

Education and Training

- Conducts formal classes of instruction, uses training aids, develops material for various courses of instruction, teaches classes in general academic subjects and military matters, and administers educational programs.
- Proficiency in English composition and speech is desirable.
- Job titles include vocational training instructor, counselor, educational consultant, or administrator.

Legal

- Takes and transcribes verbal recordings of legal proceedings, uses stenomask, performs office administrative tasks, processes claims.
- Has knowledge of stenomask, typing, legal terminology, military processing of claims; demonstrates English grammar and composition skills; can speak clearly and distinctly.
- Job titles include law librarian, court clerk, and shorthand reporter.

Medical

- Operates medical facilities, works with professional medical staff providing care and treatment; may specialize in such medical services as nuclear medicine, cardiopulmonary techniques, physical and occupational therapy, and administrative services.
- Has knowledge of first aid and ability to help professional medical personnel; background in anatomy, biology, zoology, high school algebra, and chemistry is desirable in most specialties and mandatory for some.
- Job titles include X-ray and medical records technician, medical laboratory and pharmacist assistant, respiratory therapy technician, and surgical technologist.

Geodetics

- Procures, compiles, computes, and uses topographic, photogrammetric, and cartographic data in preparing aeronautical charts, topographic maps, and target folders.
- Demonstrates ability to use precision instruments required in measuring and drafting; background in algebra, geometry, trigonometry, and physics is necessary.
- Job titles include cartographer, topographical drafter, and mapmaker.

Structural/Pavements

- Constructs and maintains structural facilities and pavement areas; maintains pavements, railroads, and soil bases; performs erosion control; operates heavy equipment; performs site development, general maintenance, cost and real property accounting, work control functions, and metal fabricating.
- Ability in blueprint reading, mechanical drawing, mathematics, physics, and chemistry is desirable.
- Job titles include plumber, bricklayer, carpenter, painter, construction worker, welder, and sheet-metal worker.

Weather

- Collects, records, and analyzes meteorological data; makes visual and instrument weather observations; forecasts immediate and long-range weather conditions.
- Must have visual acuity correctable to 20/20; background in physics, math, and geography is desirable.
- Job titles include meteorologist, weather forecaster, and weather observer.

Appendix E

Coast Guard Occupational Specialties

The following data present a sample of some typical occupational specialties. For each career field, information is listed about duties and responsibilities, qualifications, and examples of civilian jobs.

Aviation

- Inspects and maintains power plants and related systems and equipment, prepares aircraft for flight, and conducts periodic aircraft inspections.
- Possesses good learning ability and mechanical aptitude; background in automobile or aircraft engine work, algebra, and geometry is helpful.
- Job titles include airport serviceperson, aircraft engine test mechanic, small appliance repairer, mechanic, machinist, and flight engineer.

Aviation (Structural)

- Maintains and repairs aircraft, airframe, structural components, hydraulic controls, utility systems, and egress systems.
- Possesses a high degree of mechanical aptitude; background in metal shop, woodworking, algebra, plane geometry, and physics, and experience in automobile body work are desirable.
- Job titles include welder, sheet-metal repairer, hydraulics technician, and aircraft repairer.

Machinery

- Operates, maintains, and repairs ship's propulsion, auxiliary equipment, and outside equipment such as steering, engineer, refrigeration/air-conditioning, and steam equipment.
- Demonstrates an aptitude for mechanical work; background in practical or shop mathematics, machine shop, electricity, and physics is valuable.
- Job titles include boiler-house repairer, engineer maintenance, machinist, marine engineer, turbine operator, engineer repairer, and air-conditioning and refrigeration repairer.

Aviation (Electronics)

- Tests, maintains, and repairs aviation electronics equipment including navigation, identification, detection, reconnaissance, and special purpose equipment; operates warfare equipment.

- Possesses a high degree of aptitude for electrical work.
- Job titles include aircraft electrician, radio mechanic, electronics technician, radar repairer/technician, and TV repairer.

Electronics (Communications)

- Maintains all electronic equipment used for communications, detection ranging, recognition and countermeasure, as well as worldwide navigational systems, computers, and sonar.
- Demonstrates aptitude for detailed mechanical work; background in radio, electricity, physics, algebra, trigonometry, and shop is valuable.
- Job titles include electronics technician, radar and radio repairer, instrument and electronics mechanic, and telephone repairer.

Health Services

- Administers medicines, applies first aid, assists in operating room, nurses sick and injured, and assists dental officers.
- Background in hygiene, biology, first aid, physiology, chemistry, typing, and public speaking is helpful.
- Job titles include practical nurse; medical, dental, or X-ray technician; pharmacist; and emergency medical technician.

Public Affairs

- Reports and copyedits news; publishes information about servicepeople and activities through newspapers, magazines, radio, and television; shoots and develops film and photographs.
- Possesses a high degree of clerical aptitude; skills in English, journalism, typing, and writing are helpful.
- Job titles include news editor, copyreader, scriptwriter, reporter, freelance writer, rewrite or art-layout person, producer, public relations advertising specialist, and photographer.

Food Service

- Cooks and bakes, prepares menus, keeps cost accounts, assists in ordering provisions, and inspects foodstuffs.
- Experience or coursework in food preparation, dietetics, and record keeping is helpful.
- Job titles include cook, pastry chef, steward, butcher, chef, and restaurant manager.

Aviation Survival

- Maintains and packs parachutes, survival equipment, flight and protective clothing, and life jackets; tests and services pressure suits; cares for search and rescue equipment, pyrotechnics, and station small arms.

- Demonstrates ability to perform extremely careful and accurate work; background in general shop, math, sewing, and sewing machine repair is desirable.
- Job titles include parachute packer, inspector, repairer, and tester; sailmaker; ammunition foreman; and rescue gear specialist.

Store

- Orders, receives, stores, inventories, and issues clothing, foodstuffs, mechanical equipment, and other items.
- Typing, bookkeeping, accounting and commercial math, general business, and English are helpful.
- Job titles include sales or shipping clerk, warehouse worker, buyer, invoice control clerk, purchasing agent, payroll clerk, and accountant.

Damage Control

- Fabricates, installs, and repairs shipboard structures, plumbing, and piping systems; uses damage control in firefighting; operates nuclear, biological, chemical, and radiological defense equipment.
- Possesses a high mechanical aptitude; background in sheet-metal foundry, pipefitting, carpentry, mathematics, geometry, and chemistry is valuable.
- Job titles include firefighter, welder, plumber, shipfitter, blacksmith, metallurgical technician, and carpenter.

Marine Science

- Makes visual/instrumental weather and oceanographic observations; conducts chemical analysis; enters data on appropriate logs, charts, and forms; analyzes/interprets weather and sea conditions.
- Demonstrates ability to use numbers in practical problems; background in algebra, geometry, trigonometry, physics, physiography, chemistry, typing, meteorology, astronomy, and oceanography is helpful.
- Job titles include oceanographic technician, weather observer, meteorologist, chart maker, statistical clerk, and inspector of weather and oceanographic instruments.

Ship Duty

- Performs navigation of ship's steering, lookout supervision, ship control, bridge-watch duties, visual communication, and maintenance of navigational aids.
- Possesses good vision and hearing and can express self clearly in writing and speaking; background in public speaking, grammar, geometry, and physics is helpful.
- Job titles include barge, motorboat, or yacht captain; quartermaster; harbor pilot aboard merchant ships; navigator; and chart maker.

Radar

- Operates surveillance and search radar, electronic recognition and identification equipment, controlled approach devices, and electronic aids to navigation; serves as plotter and status-board keeper.

- Demonstrates prolonged attention and mental alertness; background in physics and mathematics, and shop courses in radio and electricity are helpful; experience in radio repair is valuable.
- Job titles include radio operator (aircraft, ship, government service, radio broadcasting), and radar equipment supervisor.

About the Author

Adrian A. Paradis was born in Brooklyn, New York, attended schools there, majored in English at college, and later took a B.S. degree in library service. Since then he has had a variety of business and literary experiences ranging from librarian, literary critic, writer, editor, and publisher to private secretary, hotel manager, accountant, office manager, and corporate executive. The author of more than fifty books, he has written extensively in the field of vocational guidance. Paradis is married and has three children and five grandchildren.

Susan Katz Keating, a freelance writer and author with expertise in military and national security issues, revised this edition.